Steck-Vaughn

GED

LANGUAGE ARTS, WRITING
Exercise Book

STECK-VAUGHN
ELEMENTARY · SECONDARY · ADULT · LIBRARY

A Harcourt Company

ACKNOWLEDGMENTS

Executive Editor: Ellen Northcutt

Senior Editor: Donna Townsend

Associate Design Director: Joyce Spicer

Supervising Designer: Pamela Heaney

Photo Credits: Cover: (in box) ©Imagebank, (mail, journal) ©Digital Studios; p.i ©Digital Studios.

ISBN 0-7398-3606-4

Contents

This exercise book provides you with review and practice in answering the types of questions found on the actual GED Language Arts, Writing Test, Part I. Part II of the GED Language Arts, Writing Test, writing an essay, is covered in *Steck-Vaughn GED: Essay*.

This book can be used along with the *Steck-Vaughn GED Language Arts, Writing* book or the *Steck-Vaughn Complete GED Preparation* book or other appropriate materials. Cross-references to these Steck-Vaughn books are supplied on the correlation chart on the following page. This book contains practice exercises and simulated GED tests.

Practice Exercises

Part I of the GED Language Arts, Writing Test examines your command of Edited American English and the effective organization of text. The lessons in this book give you practice in the four content areas covered on the test: sentence structure, organization, usage, and mechanics. The lessons are divided into four units, one for each of the content areas.

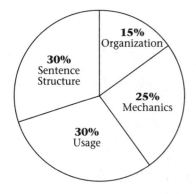

Unit 1: Sentence Structure

The sentence structure unit covers fragments and run-on sentences, parallel structure, subordination, and sentence revising and combining. Thirty percent of the test questions are about sentence structure.

Unit 2: Organization

The organization unit provides practice in making text divisions within paragraphs and documents, identifying and placing good topic sentences, and removing irrelevant ideas. Fifteen percent of the test questions are about organization.

Unit 3: Usage

The usage unit covers subject-verb agreement and the correct use of verb and pronoun forms. Thirty percent of the test questions are about usage.

Unit 4: Mechanics

The mechanics unit reviews capitalization, punctuation, and spelling. Punctuation lessons include correct use of commas in sentences, and spelling lessons focus on possessives, homonyms, and contractions. Twenty-five percent of the test questions are about mechanics.

Simulated Tests

This exercise book contains two full-length Simulated GED Language Arts, Writing Tests. Each Simulated Test has the same number of questions as the GED Test and provides practice with types of questions similar to those on the GED Test. The Simulated Tests can help you decide if you are ready to take the GED Language Arts, Writing Test.

To get the most benefit from the Simulated Tests, take each test under the same restrictions as those for the actual GED Test. For each test, complete the 50 items in Part I within 75 minutes. Each Simulated Test also contains Part II, an essay topic. Take no more than 45 minutes to complete the essay. Space the two Simulated Tests apart by at least a week.

Reading Passages

Periodically throughout the book you will see GED Practice sections. These consist of short reading passages followed by a set of questions. Reading passages also appear in the two full-length Simulated Tests. Remember to read each passage carefully before you begin to answer the questions. Reading the passage carefully and in advance of the questions may help you spot the errors right away.

Question Types

All of the questions on the GED Language Arts, Writing Test, Part I are multiple-choice. There are three types of questions: sentence correction, sentence revision, and construction shift.

1. Correction: Forty-five percent of the questions ask you what correction should be made to a sentence or paragraph. These items test your knowledge of sentence structure, organization, usage, and mechanics.

2. Revision: Thirty-five percent of the questions are about revision. In this question type, a part of a sentence or two sentences is underlined. You are asked which of five choices is the best way to write the underlined portion. The first answer choice is always the same as the original sentence.

3. Construction Shift: Twenty percent of the questions are about construction shift. These questions ask you the best way to rewrite an entire sentence, or the best way to combine two sentences. The rewritten or combined sentences must retain the meaning of the original sentence(s). Construction shift questions may also ask about joining, separating, or moving paragraphs and about inserting topic sentences.

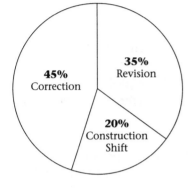

45% Correction
35% Revision
20% Construction Shift

Answers

The answer sections give explanations of why an answer is correct and the other answer choices are incorrect. Sometimes, by studying the reason an answer is incorrect, you can learn to avoid a similar problem in the future.

Analysis of Performance Charts

After each Simulated Test, an Analysis of Performance Chart will help you determine if you are ready to take Part I of the GED Language Arts, Writing Test. The charts give a breakdown by content area and by question type. By completing these charts, you can determine your own strengths and weaknesses in the writing area.

Correlation Chart

The following chart shows how the sections of this exercise book relate to sections of other Steck-Vaughn GED preparation books. Refer to these books for further instruction or review.

CONTENT AREAS	Sentence Structure	Organization	Usage	Mechanics
BOOK TITLES *Steck-Vaughn GED Language Arts, Writing*	Unit 1	Unit 2	Unit 3	Unit 4
Steck-Vaughn GED Language Arts, Writing Exercise Book	Unit 1	Unit 2	Unit 3	Unit 4
Steck-Vaughn Complete GED Preparation	Unit 1, Sentence Structure	Unit 1, Organization	Unit 1, Usage	Unit 1, Mechanics

UNIT 1 Sentence Structure

Sentence Fragments

Review: A sentence must have a subject and a verb and must express a complete thought. A sentence fragment lacks either a subject or a verb, or it is a group of words that does not express a complete thought.

Incorrect: The Supreme Court ruling on the case about flag burning.
Correct: The Supreme Court announced a ruling on the case about flag burning.

Directions: Identify each of the following groups of words by writing an <u>F</u> if the group of words is a fragment, or by writing an <u>S</u> if it is a sentence. Then, on another sheet of paper, rewrite the fragments as complete sentences.

_F_ 1. Adults in the class learning about how to make their own car repairs.

____ 2. I went shopping but didn't find what I wanted.

____ 3. The labor union council to decide what sites to picket.

____ 4. Charged with drunken driving after falling asleep at a traffic light.

____ 5. Mr. Contreras, the only resident who is against the plan.

____ 6. Plans to buy the deluxe vacuum cleaner since it is on sale.

____ 7. The state representative challenged the state-operated lottery, but his challenge was voted down.

____ 8. A survey of twenty-two cities that are considering new property taxes.

____ 9. To combat child abuse, the agency has requested an additional thirty social workers.

____ 10. To repair over half of the state's crumbling bridges.

____ 11. After deciding to go to the lake and buy the necessary fishing permits.

____ 12. The low-income housing project which will be located near Huntley Park.

____ 13. A prison construction project could employ over one hundred community residents.

____ 14. Over two thousand people attended the annual Malcolm X Day in honor of the slain civil rights leader's birthday.

____ 15. Educators planning to boycott the reduction of funds for the community college library's computer system.

____ 16. The brown shrimp harvest is expected to be the biggest in three years.

____ 17. Most of the drug-related deaths reported in 2000.

____ 18. On the way to the local discount store, seeing a video store's offer of three movies for $5.00.

____ 19. To discuss the role of women in history, a three-day conference is planned.

____ 20. The school committee member, arguing that "children have the right to know how to protect themselves."

____ 21. Soccer is a popular sport all over the world.

____ 22. When the polls have closed and all the votes have finally been counted.

Run-On Sentences

Review: A run-on sentence is two or more sentences run together. Run-on sentences can usually be corrected by adding periods to separate the ideas into two or more sentences. Run-ons can also be corrected by using an appropriate coordinating conjunction and a comma or by using an appropriate subordinate conjunction to make a dependent clause.

Run-on: Jake got a speeding ticket he will take a defensive driving course.

Correct: Jake got a speeding ticket. He will take a defensive driving course.

Jake got a speeding ticket, so he will take a defensive driving course.

Since Jake got a speeding ticket, he will take a defensive driving course.

Directions: Rewrite one of the two paragraphs below, correcting any run-on sentences. Add words and punctuation as necessary to form complete sentences.

Paragraph 1:

People who have been divorced know that the breakup of a marriage can leave deep scars on their children who often think they are at fault for the divorce and blame themselves for being "bad" children. Children are also afraid that they will become latchkey kids sometimes they fear that they will become homeless or have to live in a shelter, or they may have fantasies about the absent parent returning, or become victims of custody battles and have to choose between their mother and father.

Paragraph 2:

The credit card industry is less than forty years old and some credit cards have offered real convenience those accepting credit cards include hospitals for open-heart surgery and the federal government for income taxes. Credit cards have made debt the American way of life so instead of saving for a washer and dryer people merely charge them but do not realize that it may cost them more to charge than to pay cash. As a result of easy access to credit, many American families are over their heads in debt.

_____

_____

_____

_____

_____

_____

_____

_____

_____

_____

_____

Review: A comma splice is a type of run-on sentence that is very common. It refers to two or more sentences connected only with commas. Comma splices can usually be corrected by separating the ideas into two or more sentences with periods or by combining the ideas using a coordinating conjunction. A comma splice can also be corrected by making one independent clause a dependent clause with a subordinate conjunction.

Comma Splice: We stopped at the store to pick up some groceries, we headed home.
Correct: We stopped at the store to pick up some groceries. Then we headed home.
We stopped at the store to pick up some groceries, and then we headed home.
Before we headed home, we stopped at the store to pick up some groceries.

Directions: Identify each of the following groups of words by writing <u>CS</u> if the group of words is a comma splice, or by writing an <u>S</u> if the group is a correct sentence. Then, on another sheet of paper, rewrite the comma splices as correct sentences.

___CS___ 1. Janet decided to cook spaghetti, she filled a pot with water and put it on the stove.

_____ 2. Lucas walked home slowly, he was daydreaming.

_____ 3. Several students raised their hands, they knew the answer to the question.

_____ 4. The cat jumped on the kitchen table. She headed straight for the piece of fish.

_____ 5. The artists were hanging their work in the gallery, the opening was that night.

_____ 6. Every college student needs a computer, some students lease them.

_____ 7. Peanuts are nutritious. They make an excellent snack.

_____ 8. She rearranged her room, she wanted a better work environment.

_____ 9. Before going out, be sure to put on your warm shoes.

_____ 10. He strung up the red chili pepper lights across the kitchen, admiring the effect.

_____ 11. We bought her a lovely vase for her birthday, she loves flowers.

_____ 12. After her computer broke down for the third time, she complained to the store.

_____ 13. My grandmother called last night, we all spoke with her.

_____ 14. There were four messages on his answering machine, one of them was urgent.

_____ 15. She tried several times, but she could not reach her father in the hospital.

_____ 16. I have to get back to my studying, wake me up in one hour.

_____ 17. My little brother hates to be teased, my little sister loves to tease him.

_____ 18. The company decided to file for bankruptcy, it seemed to be the only way out.

_____ 19. Although many people were unhappy about the election results, they accepted them.

_____ 20. Being a good sport, she didn't mind when her friend was in the spotlight.

_____ 21. As final exams loomed closer, the students began to feel the pressure.

_____ 22. If it's not broken, don't fix it.

_____ 23. Before you make any big decisions, carefully assess all your options.

_____ 24. After the race, the runners from both teams shook hands.

Review: A sentence must have a subject and a verb and must express a complete thought. Run-on sentences are two or more sentences run together as one sentence. Comma splices are two or more sentences connected with commas.

Directions: Rewrite the status report below, correcting any sentence fragments, run-ons, or comma splices. Add words and punctuation as necessary to form complete sentences.

Status Report on the Search for a New Principal

To: Steering Committee Members

From: Ann-Marie Josephs, Committee Chairperson

Last week, our current school principal, Janet Malcolm, announced she will not be returning to her post next year, she has decided to take a year's leave to stay home with her baby. A special committee to begin the search to find someone to fill her post.

The Search Committee met on Monday for the first time it consists of two staff members (Bob Matthews and myself) and two parent representatives (Joan Anzalone and Lee Brick). Joan and Bob agreed to draft the job notice.

Candidates for the position will be interviewed by the Search Committee. Submitting portfolios, and visiting some of our classrooms. Also expected to meet with the staff for an informal question and answer session.

We want to wish Janet the very best. Meanwhile, we will keep you informed of the Search Committee's progress in the coming weeks. Because we want to assure you of our commitment to keeping Park Elementary School a school of quality.

_____

_____

_____

_____

_____

_____

_____

_____

_____

_____

_____

_____

_____

_____

_____

Sentence Combining

Review: Two related sentences are often joined with a linking word (coordinating conjunction) to form one compound sentence. The conjunction must properly reflect the meaning of the sentence. Use a comma to join clauses that could stand alone but are joined by the coordinating conjunctions <u>and</u>, <u>but</u>, <u>for</u>, <u>or</u>, <u>nor</u>, <u>so</u>, and <u>yet</u>.

Two Sentences: Let's vote on this plan. Let's take action right away.

Combined: Let's vote on this plan, and let's take action right away.

Directions: Write an appropriate linking word from the list above in each sentence. Add correct punctuation.

1. I may look for an apartment today, _____*or*_____ I may wait until tomorrow.

2. Computers perform many repetitive tasks _____ they cannot replace people's ability to think.

3. The woman had little hope for recovery _____ her husband believed she could fight the disease.

4. Do you want to spend the evening at home watching TV _____ would you rather go bowling?

5. The traffic was heavier than usual _____ we were late for our appointment.

6. You need to inspect each part carefully _____ you may miss some of the defective ones.

7. Exercise helps to strengthen your heart _____ it also helps to control your weight.

8. I woke up late _____ I got to work on time.

9. We climbed the steep hill _____ we stopped to enjoy the view.

10. Plants are not very expensive gifts _____ they are readily available almost everywhere.

11. I like onions _____ I can't eat them.

12. In Illinois, citizens were encouraged to spend more money _____ in Texas, citizens were urged to put more of their money in savings accounts.

13. You cannot smoke in that part of the building _____ can you have food or drink there.

14. I really like living on the West Coast _____ I miss the change of seasons in the Midwest.

15. You have completed the probationary period successfully _____ you are eligible for union membership.

16. The homeowners obviously didn't know about the flood conditions _____ they would have begun making preparations for it sooner.

17. I found a new coat I liked _____ I decided not to buy it.

Sentence Combining II

Review: There are several ways to combine sentences. Sometimes one sentence can be changed into a phrase or a dependent clause. Other times, sentences can be joined with the appropriate coordinating conjunction (<u>and</u>, <u>but</u>, <u>or</u>, <u>nor</u>, <u>for</u>, <u>yet</u>, <u>so</u>). When combining sentences, check the new sentence for correct punctuation.

Not Combined: Some people prefer city living. Others prefer the country.
Combined: Some people prefer city living, yet others prefer the country.
        While some people prefer city living, others prefer the country.

Directions: On another sheet of paper, combine each group of sentences into a new sentence. Check your punctuation.

Example: Joyce received on-the-job-training with computers. Now she's able to sell computers and train others. *Joyce received on-the-job training with computers, and now she's able to sell computers and train others.*

1. Advanced Business System's training program was very costly. Their record of job placement was excellent.

2. The police officer is very efficient. She often gets tired of the paperwork.

3. He bought a new set of carpet mats for the car. They were on sale last week.

4. Most brands of lunchmeat contain artificial preservatives. Artificial preservatives are used to retard spoilage.

5. We can leave for the restaurant soon. I need to make these phone calls first.

6. I will finish washing the windows. Could you please mow the lawn?

7. Some companies use drug testing. It is a standard part of their pre-employment process.

8. Grocery stores in the inner city and the suburbs are often run by the same company. There are often differences in prices for the same product.

9. "Happy Days Are Here Again" was a popular song. It was one of the most well-known songs of the 1930s.

10. The package was mailed on Wednesday by Mrs. Sinata. It was addressed to her grandchild.

11. The report caused controversy within the agency. It was recently filed by the Internal Investigation Unit.

12. My appointment was scheduled for the morning. It was noon before I saw the doctor.

13. The Disney-MGM Studios Theme Park is near Orlando, Florida. It cost $500 million to build.

14. General Motors' Corvette ZR1 has a top speed of 180 m.p.h. This car can go from 0 to 60 m.p.h. in 4.2 seconds.

15. Scientists R. Stanley Pons and Martin Fleischmann claimed they found a simpler way to generate fusion. Many other scientists said that their work was flawed.

16. I had a car accident when I was sixteen. I had nightmares for ten years afterward.

17. Child safety seats have become important devices. They reduce injury to children in car accidents.

18. It will stop raining soon. We can go for a walk or to the park.

19. A VCR allows viewers to tape TV shows. The shows can be watched at a more convenient time.

Review: Subordination is joining ideas of lesser importance to a main idea. To use subordination correctly, first identify the main idea and the subordinate idea in a sentence. Then use an appropriate subordinating word or words to link the ideas. The resulting sentence should be clear and logical. Here are some examples of subordinating words and their purposes:

Cause and Effect

because	in order to
even if	in order that
unless	so that

Comparison

as much as	as if
as well as	just as
considering that	

Contrasts

although	unlike
though	while
unless	

Time-Related

as	since
after	until
as soon as	before
whenever	while

Directions: On another sheet of paper, combine the sentences in each group. Use a subordinating word that expresses the logical connection.

Example: I have to go to the store. I ran out of coffee.

I have to go to the store because I ran out of coffee.

1. Mr. Johnson has to leave early. He has to pick up his son from the day-care center.

2. The hurricane had destroyed the mobile home park. The federal government provided emergency assistance.

3. Newspapers can give specific details of a story. Television news usually only reports the general outline.

4. Tooth decay has decreased significantly. This is probably because toothpastes now contain fluoride.

5. The quality of future life depends on us. The Environmental Protection Agency wants to act now to protect the environment.

6. We could save enough money for the down payment. We would still need to have money for moving costs and initial repairs.

7. I will take Mother to visit her friends. I will stop at the cleaners and drop off the clothes.

8. The new findings show that dairy products contain fat. They also contain calcium and vitamins.

9. I would like to go with you. I have to care for my sister's children while she's in the hospital.

10. The problem of drug use needs to be addressed. Many of our children will become victims.

11. I don't get home from work until after 6:00. I miss seeing the 5:30 TV news shows every day.

12. My dental hygienist is gentle and does not cause me discomfort when she cleans my teeth. I plan to continue getting my teeth cleaned every six months.

13. I will save money from my paycheck this month. I will be able to buy a new CD player.

14. The band has been playing much better recently. They have been practicing a lot and learning new material.

Directions: Review the subordinating words on page 10. Then circle the letter of the sentence in each pair that uses a subordinating word that best conveys the meaning of the sentence.

Example: ⓐ When I have time, I'll wash the car.
b. Until I have time, I'll wash the car.

1. a. Before the account is paid in full, the electricity will be turned back on.
   b. As soon as the account is paid in full, the electricity will be turned back on.

2. a. I am sure she will get the promotion, considering how well she has done her job in the past.
   b. I am sure she will get the promotion, though she has done her job well in the past.

3. a. Because the tavern was closing for the night, the customers were asked to leave.
   b. The tavern was closing for the night since the customers were asked to leave.

4. a. Even though the medication relieves the pain, it causes her to be nauseated.
   b. Unless it causes her to be nauseated, the medication relieves the pain.

5. a. Because the manager denied being at the store, a clerk saw him leave through the back door.
   b. Although a clerk saw him leave through the back door, the manager denied being at the store.

6. a. Some women said that even if child care were available, they would register for classes.
   b. Some women said that as soon as child care was available, they would register for classes.

7. a. Because AIDS is such a devastating disease, many people are becoming more cautious.
   b. Even if AIDS is such a devastating disease, many people are becoming more cautious.

8. a. Since you were out of the office, you received many telephone calls.
   b. While you were out of the office, you received many telephone calls.

9. a. Until the lottery jackpot goes over 20 million dollars, more people tend to buy tickets.
   b. Whenever the lottery jackpot goes over 20 million dollars, more people tend to buy tickets.

10. a. After providing convenience to their customers, many banks have installed automated cash machines.
    b. In order to provide convenience for their customers, many banks have installed automated cash machines.

11. a. When children are given a choice, they usually make the best one.
    b. So that children are given a choice, they usually make the best one.

12. a. We applied a sun-blocking lotion before going outdoors so that the midday sun wouldn't burn our skin.
    b. We applied a sun-blocking lotion before going outdoors unless the midday sun wouldn't burn our skin.

13. a. Telephone salespeople are annoying to me so that I'm usually polite to them.
    b. Telephone salespeople are annoying to me, though I'm usually polite to them.

14. a. Before memory typewriters were available, people had to retype whole pages in order to revise sentences.
    b. Before memory typewriters were available, people had to retype whole pages as much as revise sentences.

15. a. I don't like to eat corn unless I can get it fresh on the cob.
    b. I don't like to eat corn because I can get it fresh on the cob.

16. a. The coach let the youngster play, even though she didn't have as much experience as the older players.
    b. The coach let the youngster play, whereas she didn't have as much experience as the older players.

Parallel Structure

Review: Parallel sentence structure means that related words or phrases within a sentence are in similar form. When a series of verbs, nouns, adjectives, adverbs, or phrases is joined with a linking word, make all the items parallel in form.

Not Parallel: The leader of the group is shrewd, tough, and has power.

Parallel: The leader of the group is shrewd, tough, and powerful.

Directions: Circle the part of each sentence that is not parallel. Then rewrite the sentence in correct form on another sheet of paper.

Example: The car is sleek, sturdy, (and has a lot of room.)

The car is sleek, sturdy, and roomy.

1. The residents volunteered to board up abandoned buildings, wash graffiti off the walls, and are patrolling the park.

2. The employees were asked to stock the shelves, take inventory, and were sweeping the floor.

3. Beginning the preparations now will be better than to postpone them.

4. To prevent crime, both police protection and involving the community are necessary.

5. Mr. Cutter thinks travel is exciting because it allows him an opportunity to meet new people and for seeing different places.

6. The hospital staff asked the patient for his name, his address, and what his phone number was.

7. People tend to exercise more regularly if they do more than one activity; for example, a person could alternate bicycling, walking, and to swim.

8. It's quiet now because Josh is sleeping, Trina is playing outside, and Brian decided to read a book.

9. On the weekends we enjoy going out to eat, the shopping malls, and driving in the country.

10. Many fast-food restaurants' milkshakes are not made with milk but with fillers, flavorings, and many have added chemicals.

11. When examining a house, always check for water marks on the walls, how much pressure the water faucets have, and sediment in the pipes.

12. A small family business has a better chance of being profitable if its product is unique, uses common ingredients, and the prices are fairly low cost.

13. To live well requires a belief in one's self, an attitude of fairness, and having a desire to help others.

14. Using fertilizer, watering regularly, and making sure to weed every week can improve the harvest from your garden.

15. The Bill of Rights guarantees our freedom of speech, our right to assemble peacefully, and we have the right to bear arms.

16. Neither exercising nor to eat less food is the best way to lose weight; the best way is to combine the two.

17. Good books, watching movies, and softball are three of my favorite hobbies.

18. At noon I'll deposit my paycheck, put gas in the car, and we need some bread.

19. To paint pictures and playing music are two ways for individuals to express their creativity.

20. The special dinner at China Palace comes with egg rolls, fried rice, and you get wonton soup.

Misplaced Modifiers

Review: Modifiers are words or phrases that limit or expand your understanding of another word or phrase. Sometimes a modifier is in the wrong place. Modifiers should be placed as near as possible to the word or words they modify in order to convey the meaning of a sentence clearly.

Incorrect: Mr. Morey explained how to work the microwave oven on the phone.
Correct: Mr. Morey explained on the phone how to work the microwave oven.

Directions: Some of the following sentences have misplaced modifiers; some sentences are correct as written. On another sheet of paper, rewrite the sentences below that contain misplaced modifiers, correcting the errors. Check the rewritten sentences for correct punctuation.

Example: There's a cup in the sink that's leaking.

There's a cup that's leaking in the sink.

1. My neighbor bought the used car from a reputable dealer with low mileage.

2. The plant supervisor discussed the possibility of implementing the employee medical coverage plan during lunch.

3. We discussed plans for the annual company picnic in the boss's office.

4. I returned the defective lawnmower to the store that I had bought.

5. In the blender, the chef's assistant mixed the ingredients for the cake filling.

6. Behind the secretary's desk, the janitor located the missing file.

7. Mr. Meyers yelled at the children who were playing in the street angrily.

8. Driving in the fog, the bus driver was unable to see the oncoming traffic.

9. The caseworker in the lobby with the beautiful long hair was explaining the application procedure to a client.

10. Destroyed by the fallen tree, Jorge looked sadly at the newly purchased car.

11. Stuffed in the drawer, Mrs. Cheng found the missing lottery tickets.

12. Coming up the driveway on a skateboard, we waved to the smiling boy.

13. Containing over fifty-four software disks, Jennifer was cleaning out the file cabinet.

14. The painter began work on the rented house wearing overalls.

15. The Mississippi River has been polluted by factory waste which is over two miles wide.

16. Covered by the papers on the desk, we couldn't locate the keys to the computer room.

17. Mrs. Kaspar was waiting for her physician to call impatiently with the test results.

18. Wearing his full dress uniform, Jonathan was preparing for the arrival of the commander.

19. Disposing of the incriminating evidence, the police officers caught the bank manager who had been embezzling funds for years.

20. Elwin purchased a compact disc player from the audio store with seven special features.

21. Manufacturers are trying to produce a cigarette for smokers made of herbs.

22. Richard fed the cat holding his golf clubs.

23. Have you ever been bitten by fire ants working in the garden?

24. The building coming up on your left is the American Mutual Life building.

Dangling Modifiers

Review: A dangling modifier occurs when there is no word in the sentence to which the modifier can sensibly refer.

Incorrect: Driving to Memphis, the highway was extremely crowded.

(Who was driving to Memphis? The highway can't drive itself. The corrected sentence makes clear who was driving.)

Correct: While we were driving to Memphis, the highway was extremely crowded.

Directions: Some of the following sentences contain a dangling modifier and some are correct as written. Underline any dangling modifier, and then write a correct form of that sentence on another piece of paper.

Example: <u>Barking joyfully</u>, I greeted my dog.

I greeted my dog who was barking joyfully.

1. While enjoying lunch with my co-workers, my car was stolen.

2. Going to the hospital, the ambulance was hit by a car.

3. With time to spare, the printing crew finished the rush job.

4. At the age of thirteen, my family moved back East.

5. Walking home from the bus stop, the umbrella was caught by the wind and blew away.

6. The computer broke before I finished inputting the information.

7. Waiting for the check to arrive in the mail, the bills became overdue.

8. After working all day, the bed was a welcome sight.

9. Rushing to get to work, the flat tire on the car caused a delay.

10. While he was concentrating on the playoff game, his wife was preparing dinner.

11. Parking at the mall, my car was hit by a man who wasn't paying attention to what he was doing.

12. Wondering what to do next, the assembly line stopped while the supervisors discussed the problem.

13. Exhausted and sunburned, my trip would soon come to an end.

14. As the police were on the way to the accident, their own car was hit.

15. Walking through the discount store, the aisles were cluttered with merchandise.

16. Old and worn-out, the real estate agent showed us the big house.

17. Having read the recipe, a casserole was baked for the guests.

18. Speaking to a group of strangers, my knees knocked and my hands shook.

19. Before booking him, the thief was advised of his right to consult a lawyer.

20. While walking in the park, a huge dog bit my leg.

21. Reeling in the line quickly, the fish jumped off the hook.

22. After searching around the office, the contract was found on a chair.

23. Dangling from the fishhook in its mouth, the excited boy reeled in his first fish.

24. Circling overhead, Jack watched the vultures.

25. Walking the dog around the block, it started to rain.

26. While cleaning out the attic, an old family photograph album was found.

27. Expensive and fancy, their friends took them to a new restaurant.

Sentence Revising

Review: The GED test asks you to select the best way to rewrite a sentence or to combine two sentences. Whenever rewriting sentences is required, the meaning of the new sentence must remain the same as the original sentence. Always check your revised sentence for proper punctuation.

Original Sentence: I have a headache. I don't have time to lie down.
Revised: Although I have a headache, I don't have time to lie down.

Directions: Combine the two sentences in each pair below. Use the words in parentheses as part of the combined sentence. Write the new sentence.

Example: I want to quit smoking. I'm going to join a smoking cessation class.

(Since I) *Since I want to quit smoking, I'm going to join a smoking cessation class.*

1. The mayor was under pressure. He had to act quickly. (Because the) _____

_____

_____

2. Brett went to the Department of Public Safety office. He wanted to take the driver's license examination. (in order to) _____

_____

_____

3. The woman who provided the information was given the reward money. The information led to the conviction. (information which led) _____

_____

_____

4. We didn't have any hot water. The electricity that runs the water heater has been off since the storm. (water because) _____

_____

_____

5. I take enough time to assemble the ingredients. The recipe will be easy to prepare. (If I) _____

_____

_____

Directions: Rewrite each of the following sentences. Use the introductory words that are given. Check your sentence to be sure it restates the meaning of the original sentence. Always check a revised sentence for correct punctuation.

Example: Most people travel by car, but three million Americans a year travel by bus.

Even though *most people travel by car, three million Americans a year travel by bus.*

1. Swimming has traditionally been a popular recreational activity, but concern about safety keeps thousands of swimmers off the beaches.

   While swimming _____

   _____

   _____

2. Cellular telephones can be used for business, home, and leisure, and are becoming widely popular.

   Because cellular telephones _____

   _____

   _____

3. Cedar Point is the largest amusement park in America and is located in Sandusky, Ohio.

   The largest amusement park _____

   _____

   _____

4. Little Rock won't be able to open its municipal pools unless fifteen lifeguards are hired by May 30.

   If fifteen lifeguards are not _____

   _____

   _____

5. An increase in destructive, fatal fires in Idaho shows the public indifference to safety, reported the fire marshal.

   The fire marshal reported _____

   _____

   _____

6. The drummer in the rock band has taken a regular job, and he won't be available.

   Since _____

   _____

One type of question on the GED Language Arts, Writing Test requires you to choose the correct way to rewrite a sentence. The beginning of the new sentence is given. The exercise below gives you practice with different ways this type of question can appear.

Directions: Choose the <u>one best answer</u> to each question.

1. **Jerome is determined to stop drinking and, in fact, he has started going to Alcoholics Anonymous meetings.**

   If you rewrote this sentence beginning with

   <u>Because Jerome is determined to stop drinking,</u>

   the next words should be

   (1) Alcoholics Anynomous meetings
   (2) started, in fact, going
   (3) going to start
   (4) he has started
   (5) meetings he has started

2. **Adults can get free written information by calling the AIDS national hotline.**

   If you rewrote this sentence beginning with

   <u>By calling the AIDS national hotline,</u>

   the next word should be

   (1) information
   (2) can
   (3) adults
   (4) get
   (5) written

3. **He may never have seen a Porsche, but he's probably heard about that car.**

   The most effective revision of this sentence would begin with which group of words?

   (1) Although he may never have seen a Porsche, he's
   (2) Hearing about a Porsche, he probably
   (3) Probably never seeing a Porsche, but
   (4) a Porsche he's never seen, probably
   (5) That car he's never seen, a Porsche

4. **Rick threw the empty pizza boxes on the floor, and he turned on the VCR to watch the movie he had rented.**

   If you rewrote this sentence beginning with

   <u>Before he turned on the VCR to watch the movie he had rented,</u>

   the next word should be

   (1) threw
   (2) boxes
   (3) pizza
   (4) the
   (5) Rick

5. **The neighborhood recreation center, where all the kids gather, has adults supervising the children at all times.**

   The most effective revision of this sentence would begin with which group of words?

   (1) Adults supervising the children
   (2) At all times, children
   (3) Where all the kids gather
   (4) All the kids gather at
   (5) The children at all times gather

6. **Many people take boom boxes to the park, which angers the individuals who go to the park to enjoy the sights and sounds of nature.**

   If you rewrote this sentence beginning with

   <u>The individuals who go to the park to enjoy the sights and sounds of nature</u>

   the next word should be

   (1) take
   (2) anger
   (3) are
   (4) many
   (5) boom boxes

Another type of GED test question asks you the best way to combine two sentences. You will make a complete sentence using the words in the answer choices given. One choice should make more sense than the others.

Directions: Choose the <u>one best answer</u> to each question.

7. **He owned a pair of Irish Setters. The dogs were his constant companions.**

   The most effective combination of these sentences would include which group of words?

   (1) Setters, but
   (2) Setters, thus,
   (3) The Irish Setters he owned
   (4) companions, he owned
   (5) a pair of dogs

8. **Jessie is the best cook in the family. Everyone says she should open a restaurant.**

   The most effective combination of these sentences would include which group of words?

   (1) family, although
   (2) Because Jessie
   (3) everyone who cooks
   (4) even if she is
   (5) restaurant, and everyone

9. **Penicillin is a commonly used antibiotic. There are some people who have a severe allergy to it.**

   The most effective combination of these sentences would include which group of words?

   (1) antibiotic, fortunately
   (2) The people who use antibiotics
   (3) Although penicillin
   (4) the antibiotic and its
   (5) antibiotic and then

10. **The corner store has items that people need immediately. It is convenient because it is close to home.**

   The most effective combination of these sentences would include which group of words?

   (1) immediately, and it
   (2) immediately, but it
   (3) immediately, convenient
   (4) items close to
   (5) need because it

11. **The community was very small. It had one radio station that played only Big Band music from the 1930s.**

   The most effective combination of these sentences would include which group of words?

   (1) small therefore,
   (2) small, and
   (3) small, as if
   (4) small, even though
   (5) small since it

12. **The secretary decided to go home early. She had been feeling ill for the last two hours.**

   The most effective combination of these sentences would include which group of words?

   (1) early, and therefore
   (2) Since she had
   (3) early hours
   (4) secretary, she had
   (5) decided early to

A third type of GED test question requires you to choose the best revision of a sentence or sentences. The part needing revision is underlined. Of the five choices, the first option is always the same as the original sentence. If the sentence or sentences do not need revising, choose the first option. There is always only one best answer.

Directions: Choose the <u>one best answer</u> to each question.

13. **We don't need any <u>coffee. Because I</u> already went to the store and bought some.**

    Which is the best way to write the underlined portion of these sentences? If the original is the best way, choose option (1).

    (1) coffee. Because
    (2) coffee even though I
    (3) coffee because I
    (4) coffee, because I
    (5) coffee, however, I

14. **Elena called up all her <u>friends, she</u> invited them to her birthday party.**

    Which is the best way to write the underlined portion of this sentence? If the original is the best way, choose option (1).

    (1) friends, she
    (2) friends, however, she
    (3) friends she
    (4) friends because
    (5) friends, and she

15. **<u>Shopping at the grocery store,</u> it's a good idea to read the nutrition labels of canned goods.**

    Which is the best way to write the underlined portion of this sentence? If the original is the best way, choose option (1).

    (1) Shopping at the grocery store,
    (2) When you're shopping at the grocery store,
    (3) While shopping,
    (4) When he is shopping at the grocery store,
    (5) Because you're shopping at the grocery store,

16. **The waiters at that restaurant are never <u>friendly they</u> seem to hate their customers.**

    Which is the best way to write the underlined portion of this sentence? If the original is the best way, choose option (1).

    (1) friendly they
    (2) friendly, they seem
    (3) friendly although
    (4) friendly as soon as
    (5) friendly. They

17. **Although I like him very <u>much. I</u> don't feel like going out with him today.**

    Which is the best way to write the underlined portion of these sentences? If the original is the best way, choose option (1).

    (1) much. I
    (2) much, I
    (3) much, so
    (4) much but
    (5) much, therefore

18. **Finish your homework and get to bed <u>early, you</u> have a big game tomorrow.**

    Which is the best way to write the underlined portion of this sentence? If the original is the best way, choose option (1).

    (1) early, you
    (2) early you
    (3) early. You
    (4) early until
    (5) early although

UNIT 2 Organization

Topic Sentence

Review: A topic sentence states the main idea of a paragraph. Many writers choose to begin their paragraphs with the topic sentence. Avoid writing topic sentences that are too general or too specific. Every topic sentence should clearly answer the question: "What is the main point of this paragraph?" The topic sentence should be followed by sentences that provide supporting details.

Example:　　As the ability to type is an important skill to have in the academic or business world, it's advisable to learn how to type if you're not already proficient. You can take a course or teach yourself to type. There are several software programs on the market for teaching yourself to type. One of these is called "Typing Tutor." There are also several fun typing computer games for children. It's safe to say that it's never too early to learn to type.

Directions: Put a check mark next to the best topic sentence for a paragraph on the stated topic.

Example: Topic: How to improve your reading skills

_____ a. Always read with a pencil in your hand.

_____ b. Before the Industrial Revolution, most people did not know how to read.

✓ c. Learning to improve your reading skills could be the most important career step you take, no matter what profession you wish to pursue.

1. Topic: Recycling at home

   _____ a. Separate glass and plastic items.

   _____ b. Starting to recycle in your home is not as difficult as you might think.

   _____ c. This country produces an amazing amount of garbage every day.

2. Topic: Mentoring a child

   _____ a. Mentoring a child can be a rewarding experience.

   _____ b. Many children have no one to help them with their homework.

   _____ c. One or two hours a week is all it takes.

3. Topic: Buying a computer

   _____ a. There are an overwhelming number of computers on the market today.

   _____ b. One option is to buy a reconstituted computer.

   _____ c. Buying a computer is like buying a car: you have to be clear about what you want and what you need.

4. Topic: Dressing for success

   _____ a. Your appearance plays a role in determining how people think of you.

   _____ b. First of all, dress appropriately for the occasion.

   _____ c. Modern fashion has redefined what we wear every day.

5. Topic: Choosing a pet

   _____ a. Some people enjoy unusual pets such as boa constrictors or rats.

   _____ b. When choosing a pet, consider your budget and home environment.

   _____ c. Pets can bring joy to children and adults alike.

6. Topic: Why I am a vegetarian

   _____ a. "Mad cow" disease is rampant in Europe today.

   _____ b. I don't believe in killing animals for food.

   _____ c. Vegetarianism is right for everyone.

Supporting Details

Review: An effective topic sentence states the main idea of a paragraph and is broad enough to unite the ideas in the paragraph. The rest of the sentences in the paragraph provide details, examples, and facts that support the main idea.

Example: The metric system is a decimal system of weights and measurements. The system is based on the number ten—any number in the metric system may be multiplied or divided by ten to determine larger or smaller units. Because it allows for easy computation, the metric system is the most popular standard of measurement in the world today.

Directions: Put a check mark next to the sentence that contains a supporting detail for the topic sentence given.

Example: Topic Sentence: Anyone interested in the origins of popular music should know about the history of jazz.

_____ a. Jazz is popular all over the world.

✓ b. Jazz came out of the gospel and blues traditions in this country.

_____ c. There are thousands of important jazz recording artists.

1. Topic sentence: Pollution is threatening the home of the ancient, giant sea tortoise.

   _____ a. The Galapagos Islands are in the Pacific Ocean.

   _____ b. Hundreds of thousands of gallons of diesel fuel spilled into the sea near the Galapagos Islands, home of the sea tortoise.

   _____ c. Pollution is a big problem all around the world.

2. Topic Sentence: Many people believe that ginger helps digestion.

   _____ a. Much ginger is imported from China.

   _____ b. It has a wonderful, soothing flavor.

   _____ c. It can be used fresh or dried.

3. Topic Sentence: Exercise can relieve depression.

   _____ a. Sitting at a computer all day is a strain on your eyes.

   _____ b. Health clubs and spas can be costly.

   _____ c. Exercise helps to clear your head.

4. Topic Sentence: Adolescence is a difficult time of life.

   _____ a. Hormonal and physical changes are accompanied by emotional stress.

   _____ b. A huge part of advertising is directed at adolescents.

   _____ c. There are many programs to help adolescents deal with their problems.

5. Topic Sentence: Knowing how to budget your time is an invaluable skill.

   _____ a. Do you wish you had more time to do the things you enjoy?

   _____ b. People didn't seem so rushed and stressed one hundred years ago.

   _____ c. List what you need to get done each week, and make a daily plan.

6. Topic Sentence: Start your day off right with a healthful breakfast.

   _____ a. Hot or cold cereal is a favorite choice for many.

   _____ b. Sugared doughnuts and soda are bad for your teeth.

   _____ c. Without knowing it, many people suffer from a lack of vitamins and minerals in their diets.

Review: A paragraph has unity when all the sentences support the main idea stated in the topic sentence. When all the sentences are presented in a sensible, logical order, a paragraph has coherence.

Example: More and more people today are turning to the Internet for their daily news reports. It's becoming a national ritual to read the news online as the first order of business of the day. All the major news agencies, as well as most major newspapers, offer online sites. International and domestic news, financial reports, sports, fashion, and weather can all be accessed on the computer screen. This new way of reading about the news may make more traditional news sources a thing of the past.

Directions: Put a check mark next to the sentence that could be used in the paragraph.

Example: The world runs on energy. Energy lights and heats homes and businesses. It powers computers, factories, and farm equipment. It runs cars, trucks, trains, ships, and planes. As the world's population grows and as nations develop industry, the demand for energy increases.

_____ a. There have been power blackouts recently in California.

_____ b. Environmentalists are alarmed by the cutting down of the Amazon rain forest.

✓ c. Most of the energy we use comes from fossil fuels.

1. School is a major part of the life of most young people in America today. Most American children start school with preschool or kindergarten. They continue on through elementary school, middle school, and high school.

_____ a. Some continue their education with vocational or college studies.

_____ b. There is a shortage of qualified teachers today.

_____ c. Some people believe that parents should receive vouchers from the government to help pay for private school education.

2. Earth science is the study of the planet Earth and the ways in which it has changed since it formed more than 4.5 billion years ago. Earth science actually includes many separate sciences such as oceanography, meteorology, and volcanology.

_____ a. Meteorology is a growing field attracting many college students.

_____ b. There are several active volcanoes in the world.

_____ c. Two of the largest branches of Earth science are geology and paleontology.

3. Maps tell the story of the world in a unique way. Political maps show a country's external borders and internal divisions. Topographical maps show the range of landforms in an area. Special maps show population distribution, rainfall, and energy use.

_____ a. Roadmaps can be very difficult to follow.

_____ b. Today science and technology even make it possible to map the stars.

_____ c. Bar graphs are another way to convey information.

4. Americans are concerned more than ever with fitness and health. Gyms and spas offer everything from aerobics and weight lifting to yoga and meditation classes. Companies introduce new fat-free food products almost daily.

_____ a. Many Americans tend to be overweight and to exercise too little.

_____ b. Heart disease and other serious health problems can result from poor eating habits and lack of exercise.

_____ c. Many people work hard to eat well and find ways to fit exercise programs into their busy daily schedules.

Review: To achieve unity in your writing, be sure that every sentence in a paragraph is related to the main idea. Delete any unrelated sentences when you edit. Make sure that sentences with supporting details follow one another in a logical fashion.

Directions: In each paragraph, cross out any sentences that do not contribute to the paragraph's unity or coherence. The topic sentence is the first sentence in the following paragraphs.

Example: The United States imports about half of all the oil it consumes. Nearly nine million barrels are imported every day. About half of that amount comes from the Organization of Petroleum Exporting Countries (OPEC). The rest comes from Canada, Mexico, and other countries. ~~Environmentalists say more development of oil deposits in Alaska threatens the delicate balance of ecosystems there.~~ American companies are looking for oil resources closer to home to reduce our dependence on imported oil. Rich oil deposits have been found off the coast of Florida. ~~The problem is that oil and tourism don't really mix.~~ Vast oil reserves are still untapped in Alaska.

Paragraph 1:

The world today is full of signs. You can hardly walk out the door before you are confronted with a jumble of signs conveying all sorts of information. They direct traffic and warn of road hazards such as bumpy pavement, icy roads, and sharp curves. Signs identify streets, buildings, and monuments. On the highways, signs help drivers find facilities such as rest rooms, telephones, emergency services, scenic outlooks, or places to eat and rest. A symbol is something that stands for something else. The modern landscape is dotted with signs carrying advertisements and information. You can learn where to get a mortgage on a house, how to lease a car, or who to call to have bunions on your feet removed—all while riding a bus, taking the subway, or just walking down the street. The picture of a telephone receiver would be recognized anywhere in the world. Like it or not, the world has become a world of signs.

Paragraph 2:

The workings of the Electoral College remain a mystery to most citizens. Yet this institution plays an important role in how we choose our president and vice president every four years. Created by the framers of the Constitution, the electoral college was established to balance the power between states with larger and smaller populations. In a nutshell, this is how the electoral college works: There are a total of 538 electoral votes. The votes are divided among the states and the District of Columbia. (The District of Columbia is not a state but has a special status as the nation's capital.) The number of votes that each state has is equal to the number of senators and representatives for that state. You must be 18 years of age or older before an election to be eligible to vote. For example, California has 52 representatives and two senators. Therefore it has a total of 54 electoral votes. To vote, you need to be an American citizen and be able to show proof of residence. During an election, the candidate who wins the majority of the popular votes in a given state wins all the electoral votes from that state. A presidential candidate needs 270 electoral votes to win. Ronald Reagan won the most electoral votes ever (525) in 1984. There is some controversy today about whether this institution continues to serve the best interests of our modern democratic system. But, as with most Constitutional issues, there will be a lot of discussion and debate before any major changes occur.

Dividing Paragraphs

Review: Paragraphs are a way to organize your ideas. Each paragraph should develop only one main idea. Start a new paragraph when the main idea of a group of sentences shifts.

Example:

Few people realize it, but many languages of the world spring from the same origin. Languages as different as English, Russian, Spanish, French, Italian, Portuguese, Greek and Hindi are related. All these languages belong to the Indo-European group. The first Indo-European speakers probably lived in northern Europe in prehistoric times. As they spread out and settled in different places, their languages took off in different directions. Yet traces of this common origin can still be found. The word for "mother," for example, is *mater* in Latin, *Mutter* in German, *meter* in Greek, *mat'* in Russian, *mata* in Sanskrit, and *madre* in Spanish.

Today, as long ago, language is constantly changing. English is full of words taken from other languages, such as *solo* (Italian), *kindergarten* (German), and *shampoo* (Hindi). New words also enter our vocabulary as new inventions call for new terminology. Words such as *byte, online, e-mail,* and *hard drive* all come out of the computer revolution of recent years.

Directions: For each paragraph below, find and underline the sentence that should begin a new paragraph.

Paragraph 1:

Countless people today suffer from lower back pain. For some it is an occasional problem which tends to come and go. These people consider back pain a minor but annoying irritation. For others it is a debilitating ailment. Almost completely immobilized, these people often pay tremendous doctor bills, lose hours and days of work, and suffer tremendous pain. For ordinary, run-of-the-mill back pain (not resulting from injury or internal damage), there are some simple exercises anyone can do. These exercises strengthen the back by strengthening the abdominal muscles. If practiced on a regular basis, these simple exercises generally will relieve lower back pain.

Paragraph 2:

The American motion picture industry is one of the largest in the world. According to recent statistics, it does more than $5 billion in business every year and releases about 400 movies per year. These movies are distributed worldwide and seen by millions of people. The success or failure of a big-budget film can make or break a studio in any given year. The following are the top five highest-grossing movies of all time, worldwide: *Titanic* (1997) with $1.8 billion, *Jurassic Park* (1993) with $920 million, *Independence Day* (1996) with $810 million, *Star Wars* (1977) with $780 million, and *The Lion King* (1994) with $722 million. Today's successful films generate even more revenue in video sales, franchising rights, and the marketing of related toys and clothing.

Paragraph 3:

The history of the United Nations is an interesting one. An earlier attempt to form an international organization of nations, called The League of Nations, collapsed in the 1930s. In 1945, as World War II was ending, the international community tried again. This time, 51 nations agreed to form the United Nations. By 1995, on its fiftieth anniversary, the UN had 185 member nations. The UN performs many different functions in the world. It plays a major role in solving disputes between countries, helping to arrange ceasefires, enforcing permanent peace agreements, and monitoring elections. UN agencies also work to fight disease, assist refugees, improve education, and monitor human rights.

Review: Writing is much easier to read when it is broken into paragraphs, not written in one long block of text. Start a new paragraph when the main idea of a group of sentences shifts.

Directions: Rewrite one of the paragraphs below. Divide it into two paragraphs. Add some supporting detail sentences of your own to develop the two new paragraphs.

Paragraph 1:

What is the appeal of horror movies? Some people say that watching a scary movie gives you the same type of thrill you get on a roller coaster as you approach the top and look down. These horror fans assert that watching horror films is a normal way to relax and let out tension in a basically harmless and entertaining environment. But others argue that horror movies are a perverse part of today's culture that we should really examine. Horror movies seem to be particularly popular among teenage audiences. Many young people seem to have grown up watching films of this kind. For these die-hard horror fans, the more blood and gore, the better.

Paragraph 2:

The controversy over dress codes in public schools continues. There are two sides to this issue. Some people feel a dress code creates a more serious academic environment. Many parents feel their children give too much attention to their clothes. Proponents of dress codes say that a school uniform takes the burden of deciding what to wear every day off the student. On the other hand, many people feel that a dress code violates an individual's freedom of expression. They say that the dress code issue merely shifts attention away from real academic issues that need to be addressed. Improving academic standards, they say, is about better training for teachers and more money for schools.

Dividing Multi-paragraph Documents

Review: A multi-paragraph document normally has an introduction and a conclusion. The introduction is the first paragraph. The conclusion is the final paragraph. Introductory and concluding paragraphs may be shorter than the paragraphs in the body of the document.

Directions: Read this text on the history of computers. Mark where each new paragraph should begin. Then explain on the lines below why a new paragraph was needed in each instance. You can divide this passage into four paragraphs.

Not more than fifty years ago, computers were enormous things that filled entire rooms. They were used exclusively by the government, the military, and big business. Today, computers fit comfortably into the palm of your hand, and they are everywhere. The history of the computer's development is fascinating. As far back as 1623, Wilhelm Schickard, a German professor, built the first-known mechanical calculator. A little more than three hundred years later, the American mathematician Howard Aiken built a 50-foot digital computer which for the first time expressed numbers as digits. In 1971, the Intel 4004 chip was completed, paving the way for the first microprocessor. In 1975, the first desktop microcomputer became available. In 1980, the Microsoft Corporation adapted an operating system for personal computers, which opened up the market to the general public. Today it is estimated that more than a third of American households have at least one personal computer. This is more than any other country in the world. Meanwhile, innovations in technology are causing us to redefine how, when, and for what we use our computers. We have integrated them into almost every aspect of modern life. They are used in offices to help people find information, compose letters and reports, and keep track of business profits. Computers are found in toys as well as in high-tech medical equipment and spacecraft. In the future, high-speed access to information, education, and entertainment systems will allow delivery of services never dreamed of before. For better or worse, computers are here to stay.

Review: A new paragraph begins when a new idea is introduced. New ideas are often introduced with transitions. Transition words and phrases help writing flow smoothly from idea to idea. When writing paragraphs, be sure to select transitions that convey the correct meaning. Here are some examples of transitional words.

Definition

In other words

Order

In the first (second, third) place

Supporting Detail

As a matter of fact

For example

Contrast

On the other hand

However

Cause and Effect

As a result

For this reason

Directions: Read this letter to the editor. Mark where each new paragraph should begin. Then explain on the lines below why a new paragraph was needed in each instance and why the transitional word or phrase used to begin each new paragraph is appropriate. You can divide this passage into five paragraphs.

Dear Editor:

What kinds of parks and open space do we want in our community? This is a timely question, since it was recently announced that state funds have been earmarked for creating more parks in Union County. Our city council conducted a survey on this very question, and it's an issue about which I am concerned, too. The city council announced the findings of its survey yesterday. The survey results show that people mainly are interested in having more soccer fields and sports facilities. There is nothing wrong with this, at first glance. However, I question whether these survey results accurately reflect the needs of our community. First, the city council's survey was sent almost exclusively to people who are interested in athletics and sports. It was sent out to team coaches, boy scout clubs, and directors of other recreational programs. Naturally, these are the very people who are looking for more athletic facilities. If the council follows this path, soccer fields are going to pop up everywhere. Every soccer field will have its parking lot. Every parking lot will have its roads. All the cars will spew carbon dioxide and other pollutants. Second, I am concerned that very little was said about maintaining our current parks. Our largest park, designed by Frederick Law Olmstead (who is mostly known for creating Central Park in New York City), is a real treasure. This park retains most of Olmstead's original design. It was created to give city people a place for quiet contemplation and enjoyment of the outdoors. Unfortunately, the park's vistas and expansive fields have been seized upon by our city planners as the ideal spaces to become sports fields. I think this is a big mistake. I urge our city council to reconsider its decision before destroying some of our last remaining open spaces.

Yours truly,

Herb Slote

Review: Be careful not to create too many short paragraphs from individual sentences. Also be careful to avoid new paragraphs where they are not necessary (where there is not a shift in topic). An occasional short paragraph is acceptable when it is used for emphasis or as a transition between major points.

Directions: Read this text, taking note of where the paragraph divisions are made. In two instances, new paragraphs begin where they should not. On the lines below, explain why each of these paragraphs should be combined.

It seems that almost every time we turn around, a new prize or award is being given. There are awards in almost every field of human endeavor. Some of them are very famous. Others are lesser-known, but nonetheless important.

Perhaps the most famous and prestigious award is the world-famous Nobel Prize. It was established in 1901 by Alfred Nobel, a Swedish chemist and industrialist who invented dynamite.

He donated $9 million to start the prizes. They are still awarded today for outstanding achievements in physics, chemistry, medicine, literature, economics, and peace.

The Pulitzer Prizes are also very prestigious. Newspaper publisher Joseph Pulitzer (1847–1911) established a fund for these annual awards that bear his name. The Pulitzer Prizes honor American writers of fiction, history, drama, biography, poetry, nonfiction, and music. Pulitzers are also given in fourteen categories of journalism.

The entertainment industry has its own awards that are delivered with all the glitz and glamour that the industry can muster. For example, the first Academy Awards for excellence in motion pictures were given in 1928. This event is now televised for audiences nationwide.

There are also the Emmy Awards for television productions; the Tony (Antoinette Perry Awards) for outstanding achievement in theater; the Grammy Awards for the music recording industry; and the MTV Video Music Awards for achievement in the field of music videos.

There are several lesser-known awards as well. These include The Sprinarn Medal, awarded annually since 1914, for outstanding achievements by African Americans. The National Medal of Science is the highest science award given by the U.S. government. The Presidential Medal of Freedom, established by John F. Kennedy, is awarded every year to Americans outside the military who contribute to the cause of freedom. The Newbery Award honors the American with the best children's book of the year, and The Caldecott Medal honors the best American illustrator of a picture book for children.

It seems we enjoy giving and receiving awards of all kinds. No matter what career or profession you may decide to pursue, you can be sure there is some kind of honor reserved for high achievement in that field.

_____

_____

_____

_____

_____

_____

_____

Review: When you write personal letters, you may begin writing without much planning. As you think of a new idea or topic, you simply begin a new paragraph. When you write more formally—a business letter or memorandum, for example—effective writing requires planning what you are going to say before you write. First you gather ideas, and then you group related ideas into paragraphs.

Directions: Read the following topic. On the lines below, write as many thoughts as you can about it. Then group related ideas together. Write a topic sentence for each group of related ideas. Make sure you have good supporting details for each topic sentence. Decide on the order in which the paragraphs should appear. What transitional language should you use to introduce each paragraph? On a separate piece of paper, write your essay. Include an introductory paragraph and a concluding paragraph. Read over your writing and make any changes you think would improve it. Pay special attention to how you have divided your writing into paragraphs.

Topic: Should violence on television and in the movies be regulated by the government? Why or why not? Use your personal observations, experience, and knowledge to support your view.

Directions: Choose the one best answer to each question.

Questions 1 through 6 refer to the following letter.

Mr. Alphonse Burton, Supervisor
Child Health Insurance Plan
45 Matthews Avenue
Binghamton, NY 13905

Dear Mr. Burton:

(A)

(1) I am writing to make you aware of the problem I am having with Child Health Insurance. (2) I am very busy at the moment, and I really don't have time to write letters to you people. (3) My son Ronald has been enrolled with your company for the last five years, and we have never had any problems until now.

(B)

(4) In November I received the application form and papers for the annual registration period. (5) I sent them back to you well before the deadline of December 31. (6) I received a letter from Child Health about ten days later stating that you still needed a proof of residency form. (7) Although I had already sent that in, I sent it in again. (8) Thinking that everything was all right, I gave this matter no further thought. (9) Then in January, I received a letter in the mail telling me that I had missed the date for annual registration. (10) The letter informed me that Ronald had been taken off the health care plan. (11) I immediately called your offices and spoke with one of the company's representatives, Anita Martens. (12) She is a very nice lady, and she talked with me for a long time on the phone. (13) She informed me that I could register again. (14) She told me that there was no record of my application and documents. (15) The next period for registration with the program is in March. (16) This means that Ronald will not be covered for the next eight weeks.

(C)

(17) The burden is on your office to find my original application and documents, and to promptly register my son. (18) I even have a receipt from the certified letter I sent, proving that I sent the forms in on time. (19) I expect to hear from you soon regarding this matter.

Sincerely,
Jordan Mackey

---

1. Which revision would improve the effectiveness of paragraph A?

   (1) move sentence 1 to follow sentence 2
   (2) move sentence 3 to come before sentence 1
   (3) move sentence 2 to follow sentence 3
   (4) remove sentence 2
   (5) remove sentence 3

2. Which revision would improve the effectiveness of paragraph B?

   (1) insert this sentence after sentence 5: I included proof of my income, proof of residence, and a copy of Ronald's birth certificate and social security card, as required.
   (2) insert this sentence after sentence 5: I enclosed everything in the envelope you sent me.
   (3) remove sentence 4
   (4) remove sentence 5
   (5) remove sentence 6

3. Which revision would make the letter more effective?

   Begin a new paragraph

   (1) with sentence 6
   (2) with sentence 7
   (3) with sentence 9
   (4) with sentence 12
   (5) with sentence 14

4. Which revision would improve the effectiveness of paragraph B?

   (1) remove sentence 12
   (2) move sentence 12 to follow sentence 13
   (3) remove sentence 13
   (4) remove sentence 14
   (5) remove sentence 15

5. Which revision would improve the effectiveness of paragraph B?

   (1) move sentence 13 to the end of the paragraph
   (2) move sentence 14 to come before sentence 13
   (3) move sentence 14 to come after sentence 15
   (4) move sentence 15 to come before sentence 14
   (5) move sentence 16 to come before sentence 15

6. Which sentence below would be most effective if inserted at the beginning of paragraph C?

   (1) I am also having trouble with my son's application to middle school.
   (2) Perhaps I should have sent this by overnight priority.
   (3) Can you recommend a good lawyer?
   (4) I am wondering what went wrong.
   (5) I am angry about how this matter is being handled.

MEMORANDUM

To: All Employees
From: Barbara Samuels, Human Services Coordinator, Acme Billing Systems
Re: Recreational Softball

(A)

(1) For those of you who have played for the Acme Tigers before, you know how much fun the softball season is. (2) For those of you who may have come on board this year, we encourage you to sign up for a great recreational and team-building experience.

(B)

(3) We want to emphasize that anyone can play. (4) This is a co-ed team. (5) Last year some people from our company continued to play through the summer, too, although informally and not under the Acme Tigers' name. (6) No experience is required. (7) Those of you who are hard-hitting sluggers are, naturally, more than welcome. (8) If your baseball skills are a little rusty, however, our coach, Sylvester Brown from Accounting, will be holding some brush-up and training sessions during the next two weeks.

(C)

(9) No matter what your skill level, Coach Brown wants you! (10) Please be sure to indicate on the enclosed form what skills, if any, you do have. (11) Coach Brown also wants to have a second roster with alternate players who fill in for players when they get sick or must miss a game. (12) He needs to fill up the roster as soon as possible to see how many players we have.

(D)

(13) Second, we need to know your availability. (14) The softball season begins in April and finishes in June. (15) There are practices every Saturday afternoon from 3–5 P.M. (16) The games are played on Sunday starting at 2 P.M. (17) We play at the southeast baseball diamond at Ring Court Park on 189th Street. (18) Games begin promptly at 2 P.M. and are usually over by 5. (19) Here's some more good news. (20) Michaela Aboyo is volunteering to look after small children while adults play. (21) So feel free to bring the kids and make a family afternoon of it. (22) We look forward to watching this year's team in action!

7. Which sentence below would be the most effective if inserted at the beginning of paragraph A?

   (1) Are you a World Series fan?
   (2) Signing up right away is very important.
   (3) Spring is a season that everyone loves, especially after a long winter.
   (4) The Acme Tigers is the name of our company softball team.
   (5) Spring is just around the corner and that means the start of another exciting company softball season.

8. Sentence 3: **We want to emphasize that anyone can play.**

The most effective revision of sentence 3 would include which group of words?

   (1) In addition,
   (2) In spite of this,
   (3) On the other hand,
   (4) First,
   (5) For this reason,

9. Which revision would improve the effectiveness of paragraph B?

   (1) remove sentence 4
   (2) remove sentence 5
   (3) move sentence 4 to follow sentence 7
   (4) move sentence 6 to follow sentence 7
   (5) remove sentence 8

10. Which revision would make the memorandum more effective?

   (1) combine paragraphs B and C
   (2) remove paragraph C
   (3) move paragraph B to follow paragraph C
   (4) move paragraph C to follow paragraph D
   (5) combine paragraphs C and D

11. Which revision would improve the effectiveness of paragraph D?

Begin a new paragraph

   (1) with sentence 16
   (2) with sentence 17
   (3) with sentence 18
   (4) with sentence 19
   (5) with sentence 20

12. Sentence 20: **Michaela Aboyo is volunteering to look after small children while adults play.**

The most effective revision of sentence 20 would include which group of words?

   (1) Thirdly,
   (2) Despite these efforts.
   (3) Next,
   (4) To make it easier,
   (5) All the same,

Subject-Verb Agreement

Review: 1. Identify the subject of a sentence. The subject tells <u>who</u> or <u>what</u>. Decide if the subject is singular or plural. Use a singular verb with a singular subject and a plural verb with a plural subject.
Examples: This movie <u>is</u> exciting. Those movies <u>are</u> rated PG.

2. Singular verbs end in <u>-s</u> or <u>-es</u>.
Examples: He <u>has</u> agreed to the terms. He <u>agrees</u> to the terms.

3. Plural verbs do not end in <u>-s</u>.
Examples: They <u>have agreed</u> to the terms. They <u>agree</u> to the terms.

4. When the subject is <u>I</u> or <u>you</u>, use a plural verb.
Examples: I <u>agree</u> to the terms. You <u>agree</u> to the terms.

Directions: For each sentence, circle the correct verb in parentheses.

Example: You can ((pay), pays) by the month.

1. According to the public defender, everything (has, have) been discussed relative to the plea bargain agreement.

2. The accident victims (was, were) taken to St. Anthony's Hospital in Rockford.

3. The committee (has, have) been discussing the possibility of meeting bimonthly.

4. High blood pressure (increases, increase) the danger of serious heart problems for many people.

5. In the afternoon, I (tries, try) to be home by the time the school bus arrives.

6. There (has, have) been very little rainfall for the last two years; as a result, the drought has become more severe.

7. You don't (want, wants) to delay repairs any longer than necessary.

8. (Does, Do) anybody understand the new procedures well enough to train the temporary help?

9. As the doctor indicated, you must (takes, take) all of the prescribed medicine.

10. The new fast-food restaurant (brings, bring) customers to the old mall.

11. Many truck drivers (expects, expect) that the highway patrol will strictly enforce the speed limit.

12. Private companies increasingly (dumps, dump) toxic wastes in sites that are a hazard to community residents.

13. The citizens' watchdog group (is, are) lobbying for a reduction in health insurance rates.

14. Regardless of the reason for the attack, I (plans, plan) to press charges against the owner of the dog.

15. Parents of children with disabilities often (becomes, become) frustrated at many school systems' refusal to accommodate their children's special needs.

16. Jimmy Stewart (is, are) publishing his first book of poems at the age of 81.

17. Most people (avoid, avoids) going to the dentist because fees are so high.

18. Americans (eat, eats) 12 pounds of carrots, 118 pounds of potatoes, and 25 pounds of lettuce per person annually.

19. If treated and removed in the earliest stages, most skin cancers (is, are) completely curable.

20. From August to October in the Midwest, over 250,000 tons of ragweed pollen (float, floats) through the air to cause us allergy problems.

Subject-Verb Agreement II

Review: 1. When two subjects are joined with a correlative conjunction (<u>either</u>, <u>or</u>; <u>neither</u>, <u>nor</u>; <u>whether</u>, <u>or</u>; <u>not only</u>, <u>but also</u>; <u>both</u>, <u>and</u>), the verb agrees in number with the subject closest to it.
Example: Neither my children nor their dog is out in the yard.
2. Some words are always singular (<u>anyone</u>, <u>everyone</u>) even though they refer to more than one.
Example: Everybody on my bowling team is here tonight.
3. With compound subjects joined by <u>and</u>, use a plural verb.
Example: Brad and Jennifer go out to the movies every Friday night.

Directions: For each sentence, circle the correct verb in parentheses.

Example: Not only the students but also the teacher (is, are) at lunch.

1. All of the migrant workers (anticipates, anticipate) the end of the harvest season.

2. Each of the packages (was, were) examined through the X-ray machine before being loaded on the plane.

3. Neither the lawyer nor her clients (believe, believes) the company's offer is satisfactory.

4. The boys' soccer team and the girls' soccer team (plays, play) at the River Park field every weekend.

5. The secret tapes that contain the disputed conversation (was, were) accidentally misplaced.

6. Either the electrical wires or the light switch (was, were) installed improperly.

7. Few of the remaining parts (has, have) been examined for faults and, therefore, (needs, need) to be inspected before shipping to the assembly site.

8. Most of the employees (has, have) agreed to support the new union contract.

9. Everything, except for the programs, (has, have) been arranged for the graduation ceremony.

10. Several of the packages delivered yesterday (was, were) returned because they (was, were) not complete orders.

11. Whether the witness's statements or the evidence (was, were) falsified has yet to be determined.

12. Everybody at the meeting (expect, expects) the vote to be close.

13. Nothing, not even TV coverage of the droughts in Africa and the American Midwest, (has, have) resulted in reduced water usage by homeowners.

14. Remy's mother and father (want, wants) him to go to the High School for Performing Arts.

15. Not only butter but also many other dairy products (contains, contain) high levels of fat that can increase cholesterol levels.

16. Nobody, not even the parents who suggested the activities, (has, have) offered to supervise an event at the school carnival.

17. Both conscientious work and flexible skills (is, are) needed by a productive employee.

18. Not only Saudi Arabia but also several other countries in the Middle East (encourages, encourage) increased energy consumption by Americans.

19. Kamala and her friend Amy (is, are) applying to the same school for next year.

20. Any of the candidates who wish to attend the opening of the new senior citizens' center (needs, need) to notify the mayor's office by Tuesday.

21. Mrs. Jefferson informed the secretaries that neither the administrative assistant nor the vice-president (has, have) access to the confidential computer security codes.

22. None of the countries that signed the trade agreement (want, wants) to levy tariffs on imports.

Review: 1. In reversed-order sentences, the subject follows the verb.
Example: What <u>is</u> the <u>price</u> of two speakers?
2. For sentences that contain interrupting phrases between the subject and verb, use a verb that agrees with the subject, not with a noun in the interrupting phrase.
Example: The sales <u>clerk</u>, though he has speaking skills, <u>is</u> not good at counting money.

Directions: Determine if the verb used in each sentence is correct. If so, write C in the blank. If the verb is not correct, write the correct form of the verb.

Example: _____*do*_____ When does the new employees start?

_____ 1. The construction of the new office buildings were delayed due to the unfavorable weather conditions this past spring.

_____ 2. This month there are several items that must be completed before we begin any new projects.

_____ 3. Where was the security officers during the robbery?

_____ 4. There was excitement in the office when the supervisor announced the availability of child care services.

_____ 5. The popularity of some insurance packages usually relate to their low monthly cost.

_____ 6. The habits one acquires as a child is often hard to break as an adult.

_____ 7. What is the evidence of his irresponsible actions?

_____ 8. Do the new videocassette recorder have a remote control unit?

_____ 9. The bus driver, in addition to her other responsibilities, check on the unattended children during the trip.

_____ 10. The recent bills from the phone company shows a new surcharge on local calls.

_____ 11. Portia Allen, one of the curators of the African American Museum of Art, have purchased some sculptures done in the South before the Civil War.

_____ 12. The famous athlete, appearing at several community events, is calling for a drug-free city.

_____ 13. Local officials caught in the middle of the situation says they do not receive enough state funding to continue the operation of the drug rehabilitation program.

_____ 14. There was three people in line ahead of me at the bank.

_____ 15. Who was the firefighters that rescued the family from the burning apartment?

Regular and Irregular Verbs

Review: Every verb has four principal parts: present, present participle, past, and past participle.

1. Regular verbs form these parts by adding -d, -ed, or -ing to their present forms (work, worked, working).
2. The present participle of a regular verb uses as a helping verb a form of the verb be (is working); the helping verb used with the past participle is a form of the verb have (has worked, had worked).
3. An irregular verb often changes its spelling to form the past and past participle forms (bring, brought, have brought).

Directions: Complete each sentence. Write the correct form of the verb shown in parentheses.

Example: The phone _____*rang*_____ a lot today. (ring)

1. Because his car wouldn't start, Edwin was _____ for missing the crucial meeting. (forgive)

2. We have _____ the game many times before. (play)

3. What the action had _____ was anger the already frustrated homeowners. (do)

4. Mr. Harris, the man who had caused the accident, _____ the victim to the hospital. (take)

5. At this very minute, the Planning Commission _____ to concerns about the plan to build a new shopping mall . (listen)

6. Through an academic scholarship program, the university has _____ to recruit more minority students. (begin)

7. The proposed airport has _____ the property owners' chances of receiving fair bids on their homes since no one wants to live with the constant noise. (hurt)

8. After the press conference was over, the director of the health services department _____ if anyone had questions about the free AIDS screening program. (ask)

9. After the telephone had _____ for five minutes without an answer, Mrs. Rivera decided to check on her elderly neighbor in person. (ring)

10. The sudden, violent hurricane _____ us how powerful nature can be. (remind)

11. The mother had, for some time, _____ that the medical tests showed a promising recovery for her daughter who had leukemia, but she did not want to become overly optimistic. (knew)

12. Which contestant _____ now? (sing)

13. Because of the dangerous traffic, the children were _____ not to cross the street unless accompanied by an adult. (warn)

14. It was while he was boarding the bus to return to the army base that the soldier had _____ and broken his leg. (fall)

15. The damage to his lungs was _____ during the twenty years he had smoked menthol cigarettes. (do)

16. Almost everyone at the clinic yesterday _____ that the staff was helpful. (feel)

Review: Many commonly used verbs are irregular. They may form their past tense and past participles by changing their spelling (<u>began</u>, <u>begun</u>) or by not changing at all (<u>set</u>, <u>set</u>). You must memorize the past and past participle forms of each irregular verb.

Directions: Each of the following sentences has one error in verb usage. Circle the error and write the correct form of the verb in the blank.

Example: I had (began) a two-week diet. ___*begun*___

1. While on her exercise program, Juanita jog twice a week, attended an aerobic dance class once a week, and swam three times a week.

   _____

2. Houseplants often grow better when they are spray with a mixture of water and fertilizer.

   _____

3. Since Ivan had drove to the airport before, he knew that traffic might be heavy, so we left twenty minutes earlier than I had planned.

   _____

4. There was something wrong with the refrigerator since when I awoke on Tuesday morning everything, even the milk, had froze.

   _____

5. Make sure you knock loudly because the doorbell has been broke since last week.

   _____

6. As the ambulance attendant began to pack up his instruments, he told me it was fortunate we had called immediately since the child could have bleeded to death.

   _____

7. The police department has drawed up a plan to fight gang crime, but the plan hasn't yet been given to the chief for approval.

   _____

8. The car sank after it had went over the bridge into the river.

   _____

9. Because the robbery occurred while she was actually in the house, she was shook by the fact that she could have been harmed by the thieves.

   _____

10. I had forgot that many synthetic fabrics shrink when left in a hot dryer for an entire cycle.

    _____

11. When the recording artist sung her favorite song, my girlfriend pressed her hands against her lips and threw him a kiss.

    _____

12. Joshua had been surprised when Grandpa Myers had gave him the watch that had become a family heirloom.

    _____

13. On July 19, Norman Najimy speaked on a TV news show about inadequate funding for public education.

    _____

14. After you have finish the laundry, please go to the post office for stamps.

    _____

15. The restaurant notify all customers who had eaten the seafood that some people had gotten sick.

    _____

16. After we had eaten dinner, I had washed the dishes.

    _____

Verb Tenses

Review: 1. Tense is used to express past, present, or future time. All of the verbs in a sentence should reflect the appropriate time meaning of the sentence. Continuing tenses are used to show that action continued in the past (<u>was sleeping</u>), continues at the present time (<u>is working</u>), or will continue in the future (<u>will be preparing</u>).

2. The present perfect tense shows action that was completed in some indefinite time in the past or an action that began in the past and continues into the present. The present perfect tense is formed by using the helping verb <u>has</u> or <u>have</u> with the verb's past participle.
Example: She <u>has worked</u> here for several years.

3. The past perfect tense shows action that began and ended before another past action began. It is formed by using <u>had</u> with a past participle.
Example: Tom <u>had finished</u> working before I got here.

4. The future perfect tense shows future action that will begin and end before another future action begins. It is formed by using <u>shall have</u> or <u>will have</u> with a past participle.
Example: We <u>will have finished</u> working before dinner starts.

Directions: Write the correct tense of the verb shown in parentheses. In some sentences, more than one tense may be correct.

Example: I ___*am working*___ a ten-hour shift today. (work)

1. A survey in this month's *Parenting*

    magazine _____ that fathers don't do their fair share of childrearing and housework. (report)

2. Consumer groups say that if the U.S. Department of Agriculture doesn't hire more inspectors, the meat that we

    _____ in the future is more likely to be contaminated. (purchase)

3. Pneumonia, the fifth leading cause of

    death in the U.S., _____ a major problem despite advances in treatment. (remain)

4. Many economists _____ that people, especially those who are young, are not saving enough money for their future retirement. (warn)

5. The state highway patrol reported truck

    wrecks _____ 2.3% annually in each of the last two years. (increase)

6. Holland, Michigan, home of the annual

    Tulip Festival, _____ a competition each year for new tulip varieties. (sponsor)

7. When the politician _____ to take a blood alcohol test after the accident, he said it wasn't necessary and was a violation of his right to privacy. (refuse)

8. According to proposed legislation, the State Fire Marshall of North Dakota

    _____ that all fireworks during Fourth of July activities be banned. (request)

9. Currently, California's Wildlife and Parks

    Department _____ 50,000 trees to replace those burned during the forest fires of 1988. (plant)

10. The cost of prescription drugs

    _____ faster than other medical costs and faster than the rate of inflation. (rise)

Review: 1. The verb tenses within a sentence or a paragraph should be consistent—all present, all past, or all future—unless the meaning requires a change in verb tense. Avoid unnecessary shifts in verb tense.
Example: Yesterday, I <u>saw</u> a woman from my photography class at the grocery store. She <u>greeted</u> me warmly.

2. Clues in the sentence or paragraph often show which tense should be used.
Example: Last week, the assistant principal <u>spoke</u> at the school assembly.

3. In a complex sentence, use the same verb tense in each clause unless the action in the second clause occurs at a different time.
Example: The interviewer <u>told</u> me I <u>will receive</u> a letter from the hiring partner next week.

Directions: Write the correct tense of the verb shown in parentheses. In some sentences, more than one tense may be correct.

Example: I had _____*seen*_____ that movie already. (see)

1. Because of higher plane fares last year, the number of passengers on trains

   _____ this year. (increase)

2. By the end of next year, the current popularity of neon-colored tennis shoes

   _____ .(decline)

3. Before leaving camp last year, the boys

   _____ how to tie several kinds of knots. (learn)

4. Before this last incident took place, I thought you understood that if you broke the rules, you would automatically be

   _____ · (punish)

5. Last week, the federal government

   _____ a message to managers of professional sports teams to get tougher on drug violations. (send)

6. By next spring, most non-prescription

   sunglasses _____ labels telling how well they block harmful ultraviolet light. (has)

7. In the 1970s, many citizens

   _____ the environmental pollution concerns, and, as a result, some communities suffered a significant decrease in their air quality. (ignore)

8. After the divorce, Mary _____ a difficult time supporting the children until Frank began paying child support. (have)

9. For the last five years, Discount City

   _____ a child care service for its customers while they shop. (offer)

10. By the end of the day, the volunteers

    _____ flowers in each of the downtown planters to make the area more attractive. (plant)

11. Every week since they were married three years ago, Mr. and Mrs. Ling

    _____ at the Garden Spot Restaurant on Saturday night. (eat)

12. Next Wednesday the school board

    _____ whether to close the high school due to low enrollment. (decide)

13. When Adam went to the concert,

    he _____ his favorite band play. (see)

Pronouns

Review: 1. A personal pronoun takes the place of a specific person, place, or thing. Some pronouns are used as subjects (<u>I</u>, <u>you</u>, <u>she</u>, <u>he</u>, <u>it</u>, <u>we</u>, <u>they</u>), and some pronouns are used as objects (<u>me</u>, <u>you</u>, <u>her</u>, <u>him</u>, <u>it</u>, <u>us</u>, <u>them</u>).

2. Some possessive pronouns (<u>my</u>, <u>your</u>, <u>his</u>, <u>her</u>, <u>its</u>, <u>our</u>, <u>your</u>, <u>their</u>) are used before nouns. Other possessive pronouns (<u>mine</u>, <u>yours</u>, <u>his</u>, <u>hers</u>, <u>ours</u>, <u>yours</u>, <u>theirs</u>) are used alone. Never use an apostrophe with a possessive pronoun.

Directions: Write an appropriate pronoun in each of the following sentences. In some sentences, more than one pronoun form may be correct.

Example: I asked both of _____*them*_____ to join me.

1. Because he always complained about the insensitivity of the boss, _____ co-workers made a form for him to check off his complaint of the day.

2. Children need to be exposed to different types of music, so I'm taking _____ with me to the concert.

3. Lillian and _____ were going to the hospital to visit his mother who had had surgery last Friday.

4. My husband and I were so surprised that the children gave an anniversary party for _____ .

5. After discussing the options, _____ decided to put our money together and buy a crib for the new parents.

6. Sarah said that the missing keys were _____ and that she appreciated everyone's help in locating them.

7. The child happily patted the puppy while it wagged _____ tail contentedly.

8. Our store is sorry to inconvenience you during the remodeling, and we appreciate _____ continued patronage.

9. Thank you for offering to help me repair the chair, but since I broke it, I think the responsibility to fix it is _____ .

10. We want to visit _____ at Easter since they came to our home at Christmas.

11. Please place _____ metal objects on the tray before you go through the security gate.

12. They indicated that the packages were _____ , not the Bakers, as we had previously thought.

13. When the children came home from school, she asked _____ if they wanted a snack.

14. Since our families get along, _____ decided to take a camping vacation with the O'Neills.

15. Both you and _____ will be considered for promotion to supervisor.

16. If your new pants don't fit, take _____ back to the store.

Review: The word to which a pronoun refers is called an antecedent. A pronoun must agree with its antecedent in number (singular or plural), in gender (masculine, feminine, or neuter), and in person (first, second, or third).
Example: Mark and Amy have finished <u>their</u> lunch.

Directions: Circle the pronoun that is incorrectly used in each sentence. Complete the columns with the correct pronoun and its antecedent. The first one is completed as an example.

		Correct Pronoun	Antecedent
1.	Mr. Peabody was having trouble completing (him) tax forms.	*his*	*Mr. Peabody*
2.	After eating, the satisfied cats licked her paws.		
3.	Together they agreed to share them expenses for the repairs.		
4.	The old house with plenty of storage space and a large yard has their good points.		
5.	Both Edward and Allan have had his difficulties with the law.		
6.	Like the neighbor, Ms. Gutierrez is planting their garden early this year.		
7.	Felicia couldn't recall which box did not have their top sealed.		
8.	Neither Jennifer nor Maxine is providing their own food for lunch.		
9.	You may forget the duffel bag if you leave them in the locker room during our aerobics class.		
10.	Neither Jimmy nor Sam brought along their pictures of the wedding.		
11.	The people of France celebrated the 200th anniversary of them independence with fireworks and parades.		
12.	Mother Nature brought early spring rains, and its efforts produced thousands of colorful flowers.		
13.	Americans sure like they popcorn; in one year they ate 24 million pounds of cheese-flavored popcorn.		
14.	This computer program has her quirks but is still easy to use.		
15.	The parents were worried when them children were late coming home from school.		

Pronoun Shifts and Ambiguous References

Review: 1. A pronoun shift occurs when the person or number of a pronoun changes incorrectly within a sentence or paragraph. Avoid these pronoun shifts.
Incorrect: One should be careful of taking on more than you can handle.
Correct: One should be careful of taking on more than one can handle.

2. A pronoun must refer clearly to its antecedent. Avoid pronouns with more than one possible antecedent. These are called ambigous pronouns.
Ambiguous: She left her car in the parking lot. It was full when she got back.
Clear: She left her car in the parking lot. The lot was full when she got back.

3. Vague pronouns without any antecedents should be avoided.
Vague: Alison wants to join the union. She thinks they will negotiate a better contract.
Clear: Alison wants to join the union. She thinks it will negotiate a better contract.

Directions: Underline the pronoun that is incorrectly used in each sentence. Then rewrite the sentence so that it makes sense. You may have to change or add words to the sentence.

Example: Tiffany insisted to Jessica that it was <u>her</u> turn to do the dishes

Tiffany insisted that it was Jessica's turn to do the dishes.

1. Caroline is learning about the stock market because they are going up at the moment.

_____

2. When the teacher questioned the student, he became very nervous.

_____

3. She lost her job last week because they were laying people off.

_____

4. My brother thanked my uncle for the gift, which was very thoughtful of him.

_____

5. Margaret asked Aiyana if her dress fit.

_____

6. We never buy fresh meat at that grocery store because they overcharge.

_____

7. My older brother is a computer technician, but I'm not interested in it.

_____

8. Bradley told Simon that he had been promoted.

_____

9. I can't play that new computer game on my monitor because it's defective.

_____

10. Mary called Jacqueline at work to say that her sister had given birth to a baby girl.

_____

Directions: Choose the <u>one best answer</u> for each of the following questions.

<u>Questions 1 through 11</u> refer to the following article.

The Supermarket

(A)

(1) A symbol of America's abundance are the supermarket, which has been part of the national scene since the 1930s. (2) At many stores, the variety of produce, meat, dairy, and paper products is overwhelming. (3) In the produce section, a customer had discovered over sixty types of fruit. (4) In addition to typical fruits like peaches and blueberries, items like kiwi, persimmons, mangoes, and tamarillos are available.

(B)

(5) Some supermarkets provide nontraditional services as well. (6) For example, babysitting was being provided by some stores. (7) Other supermarkets are opening dry cleaning services, so customers can drop off and pick up their clothes when they does their weekly shopping. (8) Still other supermarkets had begun to offer space to local artists who display and sell their handiwork in the store. (9) Each of these features, say the managers, attract customers who otherwise would go elsewhere.

(C)

(10) Huge supermarkets, called superstores, not only offers food items but also sell clothes, appliances, car repair items, household goods, and furniture under one roof. (11) Critics say these superstores were simply too large for people to feel comfortable shopping in them. (12) By examining supermarkets and superstores, it is easy to see the variety, service, and convenience to which most Americans has access.

1. Sentence 1: **A symbol of America's abundance are the supermarket, which has been part of the national scene since the 1930s.**

   Which correction should be made to sentence 1?

   (1) change <u>are</u> to <u>was</u>
   (2) change <u>are</u> to <u>is</u>
   (3) change <u>has</u> to <u>have</u>
   (4) replace <u>has</u> with <u>having</u>
   (5) no correction is necessary

2. Sentence 2: **At many stores, the variety of produce, meat, dairy, and paper products is overwhelming.**

   Which correction should be made to sentence 2?

   (1) change <u>is</u> to <u>will be</u>
   (2) change <u>is</u> to <u>was</u>
   (3) change <u>is</u> to <u>are</u>
   (4) change <u>overwhelming</u> to <u>overwhelmed</u>
   (5) no correction is necessary

3. Sentence 3: **In the produce section, a customer <u>had discovered</u> over sixty types of fruit.**

   Which is the best way to write the underlined portion of this sentence? If the original is the best way, choose option (1).

   (1) had discovered
   (2) can discover
   (3) was discovering
   (4) will be discovering
   (5) was discovered

4. Sentence 4: **In addition to typical fruits like peaches and blueberries, items like kiwi, persimmons, mangoes, and tamarillos <u>are</u> available.**

   Which is the best way to write the underlined portion of this sentence? If the original is the best way, choose option (1).

   (1) are
   (2) is
   (3) was
   (4) were
   (5) will be

5. Sentence 6: **For example, babysitting was being provided by some stores.**

Which is the best way to write the underlined portion of this sentence? If the original is the best way, choose option (1).

(1) was being provided
(2) is being provided
(3) will be provided
(4) will have been provided
(5) were provided

6. Sentence 7: **Other supermarkets are opening dry cleaning services, so customers can drop off and pick up their clothes when they does their weekly shopping.**

Which correction should be made to sentence 7?

(1) change are to was
(2) change are to were
(3) change does to do
(4) change does to was doing
(5) no correction is necessary

7. Sentence 8: **Still other supermarkets had begun to offer space to local artists who display and sell their handiwork in the store.**

Which is the best way to write the underlined portion of this sentence? If the original is the best way, choose option (1).

(1) had begun to offer
(2) are beginning to offer
(3) is beginning to offer
(4) have began to offer
(5) began to offer

8. Sentence 9: **Each of these features, say the managers, attract customers who otherwise would go elsewhere.**

Which correction should be made to sentence 9?

(1) change say to says
(2) change say to said
(3) change attract to attracts
(4) change attract to attracted
(5) no correction is necessary

9. Sentence 10: **Huge supermarkets, called superstores, not only offers food items but also sell clothes, appliances, car repair items, household goods, and furniture under one roof.**

Which correction should be made to sentence 10?

(1) change offers to offer
(2) change offers to is offering
(3) change sell to sells
(4) change sell to is selling
(5) no correction is necessary

10. Sentence 11: **Critics say these superstores were simply too large for people to feel comfortable shopping in them.**

Which correction should be made to sentence 11?

(1) change say to says
(2) change say to said
(3) change were to was
(4) change were to are
(5) no correction is necessary

11. Sentence 12: **By examining supermarkets and superstores, it is easy to see the variety, service, and convenience to which most Americans has access.**

Which correction should be made to sentence 12?

(1) change is to was
(2) change has to have
(3) change has to had
(4) change has to have had
(5) no correction is necessary

Questions 12 through 23 refer to the following article.

Housing for the Elderly

(A)

(1) If your parents are elderly, you may worry at times about where they'll live when they can no longer take care of themselves. (2) Elderly parents can't always live with their adult children because of their limited space or other responsibilities.

(B)

(3) There are now many more living options for elderly people than there was. (4) In a shared housing arrangement, two or more older people, usually unrelated, shares a house or apartment. (5) This option will provide companionship and some security for your parents, since they may live independently but not be alone in case of emergencies. (6) Another option is a retirement community where services keeps pace with the changing needs of the residents. (7) A retirement community provides independence for your parents, and it also provides housekeeping assistance or home health care if necessary. (8) An advantage of retirement communities is their organized activities and programs that keep them active. (9) There was always something to do. (10) If a resident aren't able to cook anymore, meals can be eaten at a cafeteria or delivered to the person's apartment.

(C)

(11) Either of these options are suitable for elderly people who don't have major health problems. (12) Together with your parents, pick an option that suits your parents' lifestyle, temperament, and financial situation. (13) You and them can then make the right choice.

12. Sentence 2: **Elderly parents can't always live with their adult children because of their limited space or other responsibilities.**

    The most effective revision of sentence 2 would include which group of words?

    (1) live with them
    (2) the children's limited
    (3) they limited
    (4) the parents' limited
    (5) live with they

13. Sentence 3: **There are now many more living options for elderly people <u>than there was.</u>**

    Which is the best way to write the underlined portion of this sentence? If the original is the best way, choose option (1).

    (1) than there was.
    (2) than there were.
    (3) but then there was.
    (4) then was there.
    (5) than could have been.

14. Sentence 4: **In a shared housing arrangement, two or more older people, usually unrelated, shares a house or apartment.**

    Which correction should be made to sentence 4?

    (1) change <u>arrangment</u> to <u>arrangments</u>
    (2) change <u>shares</u> to <u>be sharing</u>
    (3) change <u>shares</u> to <u>having shared</u>
    (4) change <u>shares</u> to <u>shared</u>
    (5) change <u>shares</u> to <u>share</u>

15. Sentence 5: **This option will provide companionship and some security for your parents, since they may live independently but not be alone in case of emergencies.**

    The most effective revision of sentence 5 would include which group of words?

    (1) provided
    (2) will be providing
    (3) provides
    (4) has provided
    (5) has been providing

16. Sentence 6: **Another option is a retirement community where services keeps pace with the changing needs of the residents.**

The most effective revision of sentence 6 would include which group of words?

(1) services keep pace
(2) services kept pace
(3) services have kept pace
(4) services will have kept pace
(5) services will be keeping pace

17. Sentence 7: **A retirement community provides independence for your parents, and it also provides housekeeping assistance or home health care if necessary.**

Which correction should be made to sentence 7?

(1) replace it with them
(2) change provides to provided
(3) change provides to provide
(4) change provides to will be providing
(5) no correction is necessary

18. Sentence 8: **An advantage of retirement communities is their organized activities and programs that keep them active.**

The most effective revision of sentence 8 would include which group of words?

(1) was their organized
(2) will be their organized
(3) that keeps them
(4) that is keeping them
(5) that keep elderly people

19. Sentence 9: **There was always something to do.**

The most effective revision of sentence 9 would include which group of words?

(1) There will always be
(2) There are always
(3) There had been always
(4) There is always
(5) There have been always

20. Sentence 10: **If a resident <u>aren't able to cook</u> anymore, meals can be eaten at a cafeteria or delivered to the person's apartment.**

Which is the best way to write the underlined portion of this sentence? If the original is the best way, choose option (1).

(1) aren't able to cook
(2) isn't able to cook
(3) hasn't been able to cook
(4) having not been able to cook
(5) had not been able to cook

21. Sentence 11: **Either of these options are suitable for elderly people who don't have major health problems.**

The most effective revision of sentence 11 would include which group of words?

(1) Either of these options is
(2) Either of these option was
(3) Either of these options were
(4) who didn't have
(5) who doesn't have

22. Sentence 12: **Together with your parents, pick an option that suits your parents' lifestyle, temperament, and financial situation.**

Which correction should be made to sentence 12?

(1) replace your parents with they
(2) change suits to suit
(3) change suits to is suiting
(4) replace your parents' with them
(5) no correction is necessary

23. Sentence 13: **You and them can then make the right choice.**

The most effective revision of sentence 13 would include which group of words?

(1) You and their
(2) You and they
(3) could make
(4) could have made
(5) could be making

Questions 24 through 28 refer to the following letter.

Dear Customer:

(A)

(1) Thank you for joining E-Book Club. (2) We think you will find it an economical way to shop for them. (3) The first book you ordered can be downloaded following the directions below. (4) There is also an option for viewing the unzipped version of them with your browser.

(B)

(5) Here's how to open and read your books. (6) First, be aware that all items are zipped. (7) PC users needs Winzip, which can be downloaded for free at www.winzip.com/download. (8) Mac users need a decompression program such as StuffIt Expander. (9) This can be downloaded for free at www.aladdinsys.com.

(C)

(10) Second, if you do not have the most recent version of the reader (4.0), you need to delete your current version and download version 4.0 at the URL above. (11) If one tries to use the old version, you will experience problems. (12) Third, open Adobe Acrobat Reader and find where you have saved the e-book you have downloaded.

(D)

(13) We are glad to have brung you this information. (14) Thanks for being a part of the growing e-book community!

24. Sentence 2: **We think you will find it an economical way to shop for them.**

The most effective revision of sentence 2 would include which group of words?

(1) you will find shopping
(2) to shop for they.
(3) to shop for it.
(4) to shop for books.
(5) you have found

25. Sentence 4: **There is also an option for viewing the unzipped version of them with your browser.**

The most effective revision of sentence 4 would include which group of words?

(1) There are also an option
(2) There will also be an option
(3) There was also an option
(4) unzipped version of it
(5) unzipped version of the book

26. Sentence 7: **PC users needs Winzip, which can be downloaded for free at www.winzip.com/download.**

The most effective revision of sentence 7 would include which group of words?

(1) PC users needed
(2) PC users need
(3) PC users will be needing
(4) which could be downloaded
(5) which will be downloaded

27. Sentence 11: **If one tries to use the old version, you will experience problems.**

The most effective revision of sentence 11 would include which group of words?

(1) If one tried
(2) If you try
(3) If you tried
(4) you will be experiencing
(5) you have experienced

28. Sentence 13: **We are glad to have brung you this information.**

The most effective revision of sentence 13 would include which group of words?

(1) We were glad
(2) We was glad
(3) We is glad
(4) to have bringed
(5) to have brought

UNIT 4 Mechanics

Capitalization

Review: 1. Capitalize the names of specific people, places, events, and organizations.
Example: Alice went to see Dr. Jones in the Brown Building.
2. Never capitalize the names of seasons.
Example: We plant a garden in the spring and the fall.
3. Capitalize titles used with a person's name.
Example: District Judge Wilma Brown will hear the court case.
4. Capitalize proper adjectives.
Example: Elena and Charles like Chinese food.

Directions: Circle the word or words that are not capitalized correctly in the following sentences. Some sentences are correct as written.

Examples: I plan to go to (europe) next year.
My sister lives in (Northern) California.

1. The reports, detailing the difficulties encountered by terminally ill persons who could not afford insurance, were presented to the Director of the State health agency.

2. My whole family always comes together for the fourth of july.

3. Mr. Pearman, who exercises regularly at the YMCA, called doctor Jackson about the unusual pain in his back.

4. The quality of American cars has increased; as a result, the sale of japanese and german cars has decreased.

5. Florists sell more flowers on Mother's Day than on any other holiday of the year.

6. I graduated from martin luther king, Jr. High School.

7. A new bill before congress is opposed by the National Rifle Association.

8. The number of endangered species in the pacific ocean has generated concern from the Oceanographic Society.

9. Kingston, the capital of jamaica, has suffered a large increase in unemployment due to a reduction in the Tourist trade.

10. After Mrs. Ramirez's son graduated from High School, he worked two years before entering a vocational program at Rock Valley community college.

11. While he was on a fact-finding tour of rural Tennessee, Senator Millikan offered the local citizens a chance to express their views regarding the proposed interstate highway.

12. Television was primarily responsible for making the World aware of the devastating drought in africa during the 1980s.

13. Since the air controllers' strike last Spring, many Unions have increased their political activities.

14. I bought some french bread and some italian pastries at the bakery.

15. The candidate for mayor said, "There will be no increase in City taxes or in Utility rates if I'm elected."

16. My Cousin is taking courses in Biology and American History.

17. Ron likes coffee, but only if it's french roast.

18. Ben Ramirez is a respected Judge in this state.

Review: 1. Use a comma to separate more than two items in a list. (Placement of a comma before <u>and</u> in a list of items is optional and is not tested on the GED Test.)
Example: People reacted to the earthquake with fear, disbelief, anger, and confusion.

2. Use commas to separate a descriptive word or phrase from the noun being described.
Example: Joan Haskell, my dentist, has been in practice for ten years.

3. Use a comma to separate a part of a sentence that cannot stand alone only when that part comes first.
Example: When the rain started, we all ran inside the building.

4. Use a comma to separate introductory phrases from the rest of the sentence when the meaning would not be clear without the comma.
Example: For her, competition was always a thrill.

Directions: Insert commas where needed in the following sentences. Some sentences do not need commas.

Example: John, my neighbor, pays more rent than I do.

1. The Community Action Center needs volunteers to prepare food package individual meals and deliver food to elderly shut-ins.

2. Answering questions regarding nuclear waste the spokesperson for the electric company was visibly nervous.

3. Anthony Ching the union's shop steward provides the company with a list of repairs needed each week to ensure worker safety.

4. The newspaper editor asked the reporter to investigate the accident determine the real cause and identify the person responsible for the damage.

5. Until she had completed the probationary period the new employee was not allowed to use the chemicals alone.

6. To fully understand the situation the dismayed parents asked to speak to the principal.

7. Patients are taught about sound nutrition appropriate exercise and stress reduction.

8. Mrs. Landover the most active club member suggested conducting a bowl-a-thon to raise money.

9. After the job was completed the contractor checked to see if the customers were satisfied.

10. The first things we did after unpacking were make some coffee put our feet up and relax.

11. The list containing the names addresses and phone numbers of each of the applicants was given to the employment office.

12. Jonathan Welch a senator from Texas introduced legislation that would provide stricter punishment for drug pushers.

13. On the way to her job Ms. Chaney drops off her daughter at the Sunshine Child Care Center.

14. Isaac Asimov an award-winning scientist also wrote many books.

15. When spring begins many Americans prepare their income tax forms for the Internal Revenue Service.

16. Our summer garden is producing corn squash tomatoes cucumbers and green peppers.

17. Bats birds moths and butterflies help plants to transfer their pollen from the male to the female plants.

18. Agates semiprecious stones have bands of different colors.

19. Table salt a mineral is found in rocks soil and oceans.

20. Alex Longley, my accountant, has been with the firm for about ten years.

21. Swimming jogging walking and riding bicycles are all good forms of exercise.

Review: Many writers use unnecessary commas. Never use a comma unless you know a comma-use rule for that situation.

Directions: Rewrite the following sentences on another piece of paper. Correct any comma errors, adding and removing commas as needed.
If there are no comma errors, write <u>correct as written</u>.

Example: The clerk who sold me the watch is over there. _____*correct as written*_____

1. The vocational component, of Dawson Technical Institute offers a program in machine repair.

2. The woman, who identified the criminal, was given a reward by the prosecutors.

3. The carpet was completely ruined, by the flood.

4. To comply with state, health regulations people without shoes are not allowed, into most restaurants.

5. Alonzo was watching Monday, night football.

6. Erica Roberts, my mother's swimming instructor, finished her certification, just last year.

7. Mr. McArthur, a self-made millionaire, is a major contributor to the minority scholarship program.

8. Yesterday the excited bride-to-be bought the invitations addressed the envelopes and deposited them, in the mail.

9. I voted, for the senator four years ago.

10. The driver of the car, that went speeding through the red light was stopped immediately by the police.

11. Victor, recommended by his supervisor, was given a promotion to line foreman.

12. Sarah Williams was given the Outstanding Adult Student Award, for her commitment to helping others further their education.

13. The runner, who was determined to win first place concentrated on his breathing.

14. Since it smelled foul, something was obviously wrong with the milk.

15. When planting flowers, or vegetables always water the ground thoroughly.

16. Citizens, who want good leaders, must get out to vote in local elections.

17. The car with the power windows, and power locks is the one I want.

18. The passengers, and the crew, boarded the airplane slowly.

19. Rollerblading, also called inline skating, became a popular sport, during the 1990s.

20. Knowing how to use a computer, has become an important job skill.

21. Anna's friends have decided to throw her a surprise birthday party, next month.

22. I had no incentive to get out of bed that day.

23. The man, at the next table, is talking so loudly that we cannot carry on our own conversation.

24. Benjamin's aunt, uncle, and cousin, came to visit him during the holidays.

25. Jennifer, the worker with the most experience, was chosen team leader.

26. Did you leave your umbrella, and your briefcase on the bus?

27. Nekeshia and Brian have known each other since they were children.

28. Workplace, safety rules are designed to protect workers in all kinds of situations.

29. Knowing that a storm was coming, everyone in town rushed to stock up on food and water.

30. I'll talk to my supervisor, about getting a raise.

Review: Use a comma to join independent clauses—clauses that could stand alone—that are joined by the coordinating conjunctions <u>and</u>, <u>but</u>, <u>or</u>, <u>for</u>, <u>so</u>, and <u>yet</u>.
Example: Let's vote on this plan, and let's take action right away.

Directions: Insert the punctuation needed in each sentence. Some sentences are correct as written.

Example: We went to see a movie, but every seat in the theater was taken.

1. Mrs. Rashad works full time at the bank but she also attends Washington Evening School to prepare for her GED examination.

2. Nora was upset when she heard she had failed the math exam, but she calmed down and prepared for the next one.

3. The caseworkers were frustrated and upset for they had just been informed that the child had run away from home again.

4. I went to this morning's meeting with a lot of misgivings but it turned out to be a very productive two hours.

5. Doctors urge patients to develop a healthier diet and they encourage regular exercise to strengthen the heart muscle.

6. My mother thinks I ought to study medicine but I am more interested in anthropology.

7. There is not a lot of interest in today's seminar nor is there much interest in the brainstorming session planned for tomorrow.

8. They all wanted to hike to the top of the mountain but my feet hurt and I just wanted to rest.

9. I have never been scuba diving but my brother tells me it is a great experience.

10. The reason Jack is not going to the movie is because he is tired, but Howie keeps trying to convince him to go anyway.

11. The unpopular candidate tried to address the key issues in the campaign but the angry crowd kept interrupting his speech.

12. The mayor announced this morning that he did not plan to run for senator but his supporters have urged him to reconsider his decision.

13. My grandmother must leave at 6:00 A.M. or she will miss her flight to Italy.

14. Sebastian is nervous about the kayaking trip for he is not a very experienced swimmer.

15. Lawanda was enraged when she found out that she had been cheated out of thousands of dollars and she wrote a blistering letter to the Better Business Bureau.

16. I do not plan to attend the reception nor can I go to the dinner.

17. The judge called the court to order but the prosecution was not ready to call its first witness.

18. She knew the prognosis was not good but she did not give up hope.

19. Brett was proud to receive the grand prize for he had worked long and hard on his project.

20. The American Heart Association urges middle-aged men to get cholesterol screenings and it suggests a low-fat diet to lower a high cholesterol level.

21. Marilyn can return to school next semester or she can look for a job.

22. She has no plans for marriage nor does she want to have children.

Spelling: Contractions and Possessives

Review: **1.** A contraction is a shortened way to combine two words and omit one or more letters. Use apostrophes in contractions to take the place of missing letters.
Example: She <u>won't</u> drive, so <u>I'll</u> do it.

2. Possessives are words that show ownership. Use an apostrophe to show possession.
Example: My <u>daughter's</u> glasses are broken.

Directions: Insert apostrophes in each sentence where needed. Some sentences do not need apostrophes.

Example: Ten students put test papers on the teacher's desk.

1. The furniture store owner refused to cancel the buyers contract, so now he'll have to pay for all that furniture.

2. The suspects fingerprints will be checked against the computer fingerprint division at FBI headquarters to determine if she has a prior record.

3. Floridas residents are generally older than residents in the other forty-nine states.

4. NASA has decided to stop production of the super missiles since the missiles fuel tanks were found to be dangerous.

5. The local school has to pay for the building's renovation.

6. I cant understand why you dont want to work with me on this project.

7. The judge replied that he couldnt preside at the childrens hearing.

8. Unfortunately, the firefighters werent able to control the flames, and the fire spread to nearby buildings.

9. Evidently the cars exhaust pipe hadnt been working properly for at least three weeks.

10. If you hadnt called, I wouldn't have known Id won the lottery.

11. Although evidence was found that the man was innocent, its unclear why he was in the apartment.

12. Franks automobile wont start when the temperature is below zero.

13. The Congress strongly disapproved of the Presidents solution to the arms race.

14. The foreign visitors were surprised by Chicagos windy weather.

15. The court reporters missing notes were later found on her desk.

16. The familys vacation to the Wisconsin Dells scenic gorge wasnt very expensive.

17. It isnt always easy to spot deceptive advertising, but if the offer sounds too good to be true, it probably is.

18. Youll be out of town when we are performing with the choir.

19. The oil companys responsibility for the Valdez, Alaska, oil cleanup should continue as long as oil remains on the beaches.

20. Michael Jackson didnt want his sister LaToya to write a kiss-and-tell book about their family, but LaToya said, "I ll make sure the book is published."

21. My husband promised hed call, but the phone didnt ring and Ive been in the house.

22. In 1989 President Bush called for the American space program to go to Mars, but money will be the plans biggest problem.

23. Hasnt the city council recently voted to add more police officers?

24. Shes going to be sorry she stayed up so late when she has to get up tomorrow morning.

25. My sister often says, "Youre going to be sorry if you do that."

26. Many famous people dont like to be bothered by reporters or fans.

27. One of New York Citys biggest attractions is the Statue of Liberty.

28. We don't know whether the baby is going to be a boy or a girl.

Review: 1. Plural nouns refer to more than one person, object, idea, or place.
Example: I replaced the two front <u>tires</u> on my car.

2. Possessive nouns use an apostrophe to show ownership. Singular possessive is spelled with <u>'s</u>. Plural possessive is spelled with <u>s'</u>.
Example: My <u>mother's</u> car and my <u>brothers'</u> cars all need new tires.

3. To decide whether the plural or a possessive form of a noun is needed, check the noun's meaning in the sentence. If the noun shows something else belongs to it, use the possessive form.

Directions: Circle the incorrect plural or possessive noun in each of the following sentences. Write the correct form in the blank after each sentence.

Example: My (sisters) cat is gray. _____*sister's*_____

1. The mothers youngest child was the only one who had problems with his teeth.

   _____

2. Students in China demonstrated to press the government to institute civil rights' such as freedom of speech.

   _____

3. The governments proposed funding cuts of veterans services has angered many Vietnam veterans.

   _____

4. The man asked his childrens permission to remarry to let them know that their opinions were important to him.

   _____

5. Governor Lujans plan to attract business by providing companies with tax incentives was applauded by the Better Business Association.

   _____

6. While following the deers trail, the three hunters recounted stories about memorable previous hunts.

   _____

7. The optometrist will test each eyes vision separately before she prescribes glasses or contact lenses.

   _____

8. A new state law protects public employees who expose co-workers fraudulent practices from threats or retaliation by the employer.

   _____

9. After the searcher's located the missing people, the Red Cross provided emergency medical attention and warm blankets.

   _____

10. Yesterdays Transit Authority agreement changes four bus routes in order to better serve the communities surrounding Chicago.

    _____

11. Sunshine Food Market's prices are always lower than other grocery stores prices.

    _____

12. Harry accidentally dropped one of the bookcases glass shelves while he was unpacking the cartons.

    _____

13. The crash's impact completely destroyed the engine of the car, but fortunately the passengers' weren't seriously injured.

    _____

14. The childrens health and safety must be the first concern of all day-care centers.

    _____

Review: 1. Homonyms are words that sound alike but have different spellings and meanings. Here is a list of some commonly confused homonyms.

board: a piece of wood	bored: not interested
brake: to stop	break: to damage or destroy, a rest period
feat: achievement	feet: plural of *foot*
hear: to listen	here: in this place
hole: opening	whole: entire
knew: past tense of *know*	new: latest, additional
passed: went by	past: a time before
principal: main, or head of a school	principle: rule, belief

2. Some words are not actual homonyms, but they are often confused because they sound so similar.

accept: to receive or get	except: excluding
affect: to influence	effect: a result

Directions: Insert the correct word from the lists above in the blank in each of the following sentences.

Example: We've decided to set up camp right _____ *here* _____.

1. The teacher talked on and on while the students sat there, completely _____.

2. From the moment we met, we felt as if we had known each other our _____ lives.

3. Climbing Mount Everest was an incredible _____ of courage.

4. Time _____ slowly by as the snow fell and the city grew silent.

5. The _____ of our school won an award for leadership.

6. The _____ shipment of sneakers was sold out almost as soon as it arrived.

7. In the _____, it was not unusual for women to stay home while men went out and worked.

8. Scientists at NASA study how microgravity can _____ living things.

9. "_____ what I have to say before you make up your minds," the candidate said.

10. The sign in the china shop said, "If you _____ it, you pay for it."

11. The detective discovered the money stashed in a _____ in the floor.

12. If you _____ what I know, you wouldn't say that.

13. People felt the candidate was a man of _____ and integrity.

14. Doctors warn smokers of the long-term _____ cigarettes have on health.

15. The driver put his foot on the _____ as he saw the child run into the street.

16. He was not there to _____ his award in person.

17. "_____ is the spot where I buried the treasure!" the pirate exclaimed.

18. After wearing her new shoes all day long, her _____ were killing her.

Review: Some contractions and possessives are homonyms.

<u>It's</u>: a contraction of the pronoun <u>it</u> and the verb <u>is</u> or <u>has</u>
<u>Its</u>: a possessive pronoun showing ownership

<u>They're</u>: a contraction of the pronoun <u>they</u> and the verb <u>are</u>
<u>There</u>: an adverb that shows direction
<u>Their</u>: a possessive pronoun that shows ownership

<u>Who's</u>: a contraction of the pronoun <u>who</u> and the verb <u>is</u> or <u>has</u>
<u>Whose</u>: a pronoun showing possession

<u>You're</u>: a contraction of the pronoun <u>you</u> and the verb <u>are</u>
<u>Your</u>: a possessive pronoun

Directions: Write the correct word from the list above in each sentence.

Example: You're going to need _____*your*_____ umbrella today.

1. The store that sells only cookies will open

   _____ third site next week in the mall.

2. The person _____ responsible has not yet been identified.

3. _____ very fortunate that she was offered a scholarship; she wouldn't have been able to attend otherwise.

4. Due to their past involvement,

   _____ being asked to help the new volunteers learn their responsibilities.

5. The packing crates we need are over

   _____ by the wall.

6. The child _____ parents encourage good study habits usually does well in school.

7. Please bring _____ suggestions regarding safety to the next meeting.

8. The McDonald family took

   _____ dog with them when they went to visit Mrs. McDonald's mother in Florida.

9. _____ being asked to bring a dish for your company picnic.

10. While good nutrition is important,

    _____ also necessary to get an adequate amount of exercise.

11. To register for any job listed on the board,

    you must have _____ social security card with you.

12. The actor _____ most popular at any given time usually has a special, innocent look about him or her.

13. The couple asked _____ real estate agent to recommend the best way to finance a house within their budget.

14. Because _____ so organized, they can get a lot accomplished each day.

15. When the doctor arrived at the emergency room, her patient had already been waiting

    _____ for over an hour.

16. Can you tell _____ handwriting this is?

17. The builders don't know yet when

    _____ going to begin construction.

Directions: Choose the <u>one best answer</u> for each question.

<u>Questions 1 through 10</u> refer to the following article.

Understanding Insomnia

(A)

(1) Whose most likely to suffer from insomnia? (2) Nearly everyone has an occasional problem falling asleep and many people suffer chronically. (3) Insomnia, once thought to be psychological is now believed to have physical causes. (4) Physical causes of insomnia include pain use of nasal decongestants, and drinking too much alcohol.

(B)

(5) Doctors recommend several actions for people who suffer from insomnia. (6) These steps include exercising vigorously avoiding daytime naps, and relaxing before bed. (7) Hypnosis has also been used with success.

(C)

(8) No specialist on sleeping disorders recommends long-term use of sleeping pills. (9) Pills only mask whatever problem is causing sleeplessness and are potentially addicting. (10) Pills also decrease the quality of sleep, by not allowing the body to sink into deep sleep levels. (11) There are different levels of sleep that everyone needs to go through each time we fall asleep. (12) One level is called REM, or rapid eye movement, sleep. (13) This is the dreaming level, and a persons eyes move behind closed eyelids as if they were watching a movie.

(D)

(14) In the passed, insomnia was often thought to be incurable. (15) Today we know it can be cured—with time and patience.

1. Sentence 1: **Whose most likely to suffer from insomnia?**

   Which correction should be made to sentence 1?

   (1) change <u>Whose</u> to <u>Who's</u>
   (2) change <u>Whose</u> to <u>Who</u>
   (3) insert a comma after <u>suffer</u>
   (4) insert a comma after <u>from</u>
   (5) no correction is necessary

2. Sentence 2: **Nearly everyone has an occasional problem falling <u>asleep and</u> many people suffer chronically.**

   Which is the best way to write the underlined portion of this sentence? If the original is the best way, choose option (1).

   (1) asleep and
   (2) asleep. And
   (3) asleep, and
   (4) asleep, therefore,
   (5) asleep, instead

3. Sentence 3: **Insomnia, once thought to be psychological is now believed to have physical causes.**

   Which correction should be made to sentence 3?

   (1) remove the comma after <u>Insomnia</u>
   (2) insert a comma after <u>psychological</u>
   (3) insert a comma after <u>now</u>
   (4) insert a comma after <u>believed</u>
   (5) no correction is necessary

4. Sentence 4: **Physical causes of insomnia <u>include pain use of</u> nasal decongestants, and drinking too much alcohol.**

   Which is the best way to write the underlined portion of this sentence? If the original is the best way, choose option (1).

   (1) include pain use of
   (2) include pain, use, of
   (3) include, pain, and use of
   (4) include pain, use of
   (5) including pain, and the use of

5. Sentence 6: **These steps include <u>exercising vigorously avoiding</u> daytime naps, and relaxing before bed.**

   Which is the best way to write the underlined portion of this sentence? If the original is the best way, choose option (1).

   (1) exercising vigorously avoiding
   (2) exercising vigorously, avoiding
   (3) exercising, vigorously avoiding
   (4) to exercise vigorously avoiding,
   (5) exercising vigorously. Avoiding

6. Sentence 8: **No specialist on sleeping disorders recommends long-term use of sleeping pills.**

   Which correction should be made to sentence 8?

   (1) insert a comma after <u>specialist</u>
   (2) insert a comma after <u>disorders</u>
   (3) insert a comma after <u>recommends</u>
   (4) insert a comma after <u>use</u>
   (5) no correction is necessary

7. Sentence 9: **Pills only mask whatever problem is causing sleeplessness and are potentially addicting.**

   Which correction should be made to sentence 9?

   (1) change <u>Pills</u> to <u>Pill's</u>
   (2) insert a comma after <u>Pills</u>
   (3) insert a comma after <u>mask</u>
   (4) insert a comma after <u>sleeplessness</u>
   (5) no correction is necessary

8. Sentence 10: **Pills also decrease the quality of <u>sleep, by not allowing</u> the body to sink into deep sleep levels.**

   Which is the best way to write the underlined portion of this sentence? If the original is the best way, choose option (1).

   (1) sleep, by not allowing
   (2) sleep. by not allowing
   (3) sleep by not allowing
   (4) sleep but do not allow
   (5) sleep, but do not allow

9. Sentence 13: **This is the dreaming level, and a persons eyes move behind closed eyelids as if they were watching a movie.**

   Which correction should be made to sentence 13?

   (1) remove the comma after <u>level</u>
   (2) change <u>persons</u> to <u>person's</u>
   (3) insert a comma after <u>eyelids</u>
   (4) change <u>movie</u> to <u>Movie</u>
   (5) no correction is necessary

10. Sentence 14: **<u>In the passed, insomnia</u> was often thought to be incurable.**

    Which is the best way to write the underlined portion of this sentence? If the original is best way, choose option (1).

    (1) In the passed, insomnia
    (2) In the passed insomnia
    (3) In the past insomnia
    (4) In the past, insomnia
    (5) In the Past, insomnia

Questions 11 through 22 refer to the following article.

Redwoods: Our National Treasure

(A)

(1) California's redwood trees the tallest living things on Earth, stand over 300 feet tall. (2) Some of them were young sprouts when the Vikings sailed to america. (3) Redwood trees are also known as sequoias or giant sequoias. (4) Redwoods covered vast areas of our planet 40 Million years ago. (5) Now they can only be found along, the West coast.

(B)

(6) Numerous preserves have been established to save the redwoods. (7) These preserves have, of coarse, become a major tourist attraction. (8) The Redwood National Park in northern California attracts many visitors each summer. (9) The tourists arrive by bus, but they must walk the last 1.4 miles to see the trees. (10) There efforts are rewarded, however, with vistas of huge granite mountains and deep canyons. (11) The parks beautiful trees keep tourists coming back year after year.

(C)

(12) One tree in particular the General Sherman Tree, is estimated to be one of the oldest living things on Earth. (13) Scientists believe this tree, which is 36.5 feat in diameter, is more than 3,500 years old. (14) It is truly a wonder to behold.

(D)

(15) In California, laws have been past to protect the redwoods and preserve their beauty for generations. (16) Once cut down, these national treasures can never be replaced.

11. Sentence 1: **California's redwood trees the tallest living things on Earth, stand over 300 feet tall.**

    Which correction should be made to sentence 1?

    (1) change California's to Californias
    (2) insert a comma after trees
    (3) insert a comma after things
    (4) remove the comma after Earth
    (5) no correction is necessary

12. Sentence 2: **Some of them were young sprouts when the Vikings sailed to america.**

    Which correction should be made to sentence 2?

    (1) insert a comma after them
    (2) insert a comma after sprouts
    (3) change america to America
    (4) change Vikings to vikings
    (5) no correction is necessary

13. Sentence 4: **Redwoods covered vast areas of our planet 40 Million years ago.**

    Which correction should be made to sentence 4?

    (1) change Redwoods to Redwood's
    (2) insert a comma after areas
    (3) insert a comma after planet
    (4) change Million to million
    (5) no correction is necessary

14. Sentence 5: **Now they can only be found along, the West coast.**

    Which correction should be made to sentence 5?

    (1) insert a comma after Now
    (2) insert a semicolon after found
    (3) remove the comma after along
    (4) insert a comma after the
    (5) no correction is necessary

15. Sentence 6: **Numerous preserves have been established to save the redwoods.**

    Which correction should be made to sentence 6?

    (1) change preserves to Preserves
    (2) insert a comma after preserves
    (3) insert a comma after established
    (4) change redwoods to Redwoods
    (5) no correction is necessary

16. Sentence 7: **These <u>preserves have, of coarse, become</u> a major tourist attraction.**

    Which is the best way to write the underlined portion of this sentence? If the original is best way, choose option (1).

    (1) preserves have, of coarse, become
    (2) preserves, have of coarse become
    (3) preserves have, of course, become
    (4) preserves, have, of coarse, become
    (5) preserves have of coarse, become

17. Sentence 9: **The tourists <u>arrive by bus, but</u> they must walk the last 1.4 miles to see the trees.**

    Which is the best way to write the underlined portion of this sentence? If the original is best way, choose option (1).

    (1) arrive by bus, but
    (2) arrive by bus but
    (3) arrive, by bus but
    (4) arrive by bus but,
    (5) arrive by, bus but

18. Sentence 10: **<u>There efforts are rewarded, however,</u> with vistas of huge granite mountains and deep canyons.**

    Which is the best way to write the underlined portion of this sentence? If the original is best way, choose option (1).

    (1) There efforts are rewarded, however,
    (2) Their efforts are rewarded, however,
    (3) They're efforts are rewarded, however,
    (4) There efforts are rewarded however,
    (5) Their efforts are rewarded however,

19. Sentence 11: **The parks beautiful trees keep tourists coming back year after year.**

    Which correction should be made to sentence 11?

    (1) change <u>parks</u> to <u>park's</u>
    (2) change <u>parks</u> to <u>parks'</u>
    (3) insert a comma after <u>trees</u>
    (4) insert a comma after <u>back</u>
    (5) no correction is necessary

20. Sentence 12: **One tree in particular the General Sherman Tree, is estimated to be one of the oldest living things on Earth.**

    Which correction should be made to sentence 12?

    (1) insert a comma after <u>particular</u>
    (2) remove the comma after <u>Tree</u>
    (3) insert a comma after <u>estimated</u>
    (4) insert a comma after <u>be</u>
    (5) no correction is necessary

21. Sentence 13: **Scientists believe this tree, which is 36.5 feat in diameter, is more than 3,500 years old.**

    Which correction should be made to sentence 13?

    (1) insert a comma after <u>believe</u>
    (2) remove the comma after <u>tree</u>
    (3) replace <u>feat</u> with <u>feet</u>
    (4) remove the comma after <u>diameter</u>
    (5) no correction is necessary

22. Sentence 15: **In California, laws have been past to protect the redwoods and preserve their beauty for generations.**

    Which correction should be made to sentence 15?

    (1) change <u>California</u> to <u>california</u>
    (2) replace <u>past</u> with <u>passed</u>
    (3) insert a comma after <u>past</u>
    (4) insert a comma after <u>redwoods</u>
    (5) no correction is necessary

LANGUAGE ARTS, WRITING, Part I

Directions

The Language Arts, Writing Simulated Test A is intended to measure your ability to use clear and effective English. It is a test of English as it should be written, not as it might be spoken.

This test consists of paragraphs with numbered sentences. Some of the sentences contain errors in sentence structure, organization, usage, or mechanics (spelling, punctuation, and capitalization). After reading the numbered sentences, answer the multiple choice questions that follow. Some questions refer to sentences that are correct as written. The best answer for these questions is the one that leaves the sentence as originally written. The best answer for some questions is the one that produces a sentence that is consistent with the verb tense and point of view used throughout the paragraph.

You should spend no more than 75 minutes answering the 50 questions on this test. Work carefully, but do not spend too much time on any one question. Do not skip any items. Make a reasonable guess when you are not sure of an answer. You will not be penalized for incorrect answers.

When time is up, mark the last item you finished. This will tell you whether you can finish the real GED Test in the time allowed. Then complete the test.

Record your answers to the questions on a copy of the answer sheet on page 110. Be sure that all required information is properly recorded on the answer sheet.

To record your answers, fill in the numbered space on the answer sheet that corresponds to the answer you choose for each question on the test.

Example:

Sentence 1: **We were all honored to meet governor Phillips.**

What correction should be made to sentence 1?

(1) change <u>honored</u> to <u>honoring</u>
(2) insert a comma after <u>honored</u>
(3) change <u>meet</u> to <u>met</u>
(4) change <u>governor</u> to <u>Governor</u>
(5) no correction is necessary   ① ② ③ ● ⑤

In this example, the word <u>governor</u> should be capitalized; therefore, answer space 4 would be marked on the answer sheet.

Do not rest the point of your pencil on the answer sheet while you are considering your answer. Make no stray or unnecessary marks. If you change an answer, erase your first mark completely. Mark only one answer space for each question; multiple answers will be scored as incorrect. Do not fold or crease your answer sheet.

When you finish the test, use the Analysis of Performance Chart on page 76 to determine whether you are ready to take the real GED Test and, if not, which skill areas need additional review.

Adapted with permission of the American Council on Education.

Directions: Choose the one best answer to each question.

Questions 1 through 7 refer to the following article.

Circuit Boards

(A)

(1) Almost all electronic appliances, from microwave ovens to videocassette recorders, uses circuit boards. (2) Circuit boards, vary in complexity, but all contain instruction panels composed of integrated circuits, resistors, capacitors, and other electrical components. (3) These components are connected by conducting paths. (4) The panels tell the machine what to do by conducting electrical current along pathways. (5) These boards were manufactured by using highly toxic acids to conduct electricity over copper-coated panels. (6) When the boards are overused. (7) The copper becomes overheated and stops the electrical current. (8) This is the most common cause of malfunctions n household appliances.

(B)

(9) Researchers have been looking for a new way to manufacture circuit boards that would eliminate this kind of problem. (10) A new technology that uses an alloy ink to "print" the pathways are being tested. (11) Sometimes there are unexpected benefits to new technologies. (12) One unexpected benefit of this particular technology is that boards could be "printed" on fabrics and other flexible materials. (13) This could have some interesting applications. 14) For example, medical devices that monitor heart rate could be "printed" on shirts, blouses, or dresses. (15) Clothes that beam light could be the fashion of the future! (16) The application of this technology will be limited only by scientists creativity.

1. Sentence 1: **Almost all electronic appliances, from microwave ovens to videocassette recorders, uses circuit boards.**

   Which correction should be made to sentence 1?

   (1) replace all with each
   (2) insert a comma after all
   (3) remove the comma after appliances
   (4) change uses to use
   (5) no correction is necessary

2. Sentence 2: **Circuit boards, vary in complexity, but all contain instruction panels composed of integrated circuits, resistors, capacitors, and other electrical components.**

   Which correction should be made to sentence 2?

   (1) remove the comma after boards
   (2) change vary to varies
   (3) change contain to contains
   (4) insert a comma after other
   (5) no correction is necessary

3. Sentence 5: **These boards <u>were manufactured</u> by using highly toxic acids to conduct electricity over copper-coated panels.**

   Which is the best way to write the underlined portion of this sentence? If you think the original is the best way, choose option (1).

   (1) were manufactured
   (2) are manufactured
   (3) is manufactured
   (4) has been manufactured
   (5) will be manufactured

4. Sentences 6 and 7: **When the boards are <u>overused. The copper</u> becomes overheated and stops the electrical current.**

   Which is the best way to write the underlined portion of these sentences? If the original is the best way, choose option (1).

   (1) overused. The copper
   (2) overused the copper
   (3) overused so the copper
   (4) overused and the copper
   (5) overused, the copper

5. Sentence 9: **Researchers have been looking for a new way to manufacture circuit boards that would eliminate this kind of problem.**

   Which revision would improve the effectiveness of the article?

   (1) move sentence 9 to follow sentence 3
   (2) move sentence 9 to follow sentence 12
   (3) move sentence 9 to the end of paragraph A
   (4) move sentence 9 to the end of paragraph B
   (5) no revision is necessary

6. Sentence 10: **A new technology that uses an alloy ink to "print" the pathways <u>are being tested</u>.**

   Which is the best way to write the underlined portion of this sentence? If the original is the best way, choose option (1).

   (1) are being tested.
   (2) is being tested.
   (3) should have been tested.
   (4) have been tested.
   (5) were being tested.

7. Sentence 16: **The application of this technology will be limited only by scientists creativity.**

   Which correction should be made to sentence 16?

   (1) replace <u>will</u> with <u>would</u>
   (2) insert a comma after <u>limited</u>
   (3) change <u>scientists</u> to <u>scientist's</u>
   (4) change <u>scientists</u> to <u>scientists'</u>
   (5) no correction is necessary

Questions 8 through 16 refer to the following article.

Liquid Diets

(A)

(1) Liquid protein diets promise obese Americans a way to take weight off fast. (2) No solid food eaten, but the dieter may drink up to five protein supplements per day. (3) These diets, which provide fewer than 800 calories a day should be undertaken only under proper medical supervision. (4) The average weight loss, according to doctors who use the diets to treat overweight patients, is about 60 pounds in 6 months. (5) The diet drinks are only available through hospital-based programs where all patients' blood pressures, heart rates, and blood chemistries are checked at least twice a month to monitor his health condition. (6) There are some serious drawbacks to these diets. (7) A typical program costs at least $100 per week, bringing the total cost of the program to over $2,000. (8) Problems can include fatigue, dry skin, diarrhea, chills, and muscle cramps. (9) All of these side affects are reversible once the patient starts eating again.

(B)

(10) After the fast, most programs encourage dieters for at least a year to enter a maintenance phase. (11) During this phase, they receive follow-up assistance to keep the weight off. (12) To be admitted to a program a person generally has to be at least 40 pounds overweight. (13) It is crucial that individuals who are interested in a fasting diet check with there physician prior to beginning a program.

8. Sentence 2: **No solid food eaten, but the dieter may drink up to five protein supplements per day.**

   Which is the best way to write the underlined portion of this sentence? If the original is the best way, choose option (1).

   (1) food eaten, but
   (2) food are eaten, but
   (3) food was eaten, but
   (4) food is eaten, but
   (5) food has been eaten, but

9. Sentence 3: **These diets, which provide fewer than 800 calories a day should be undertaken only under proper medical supervision.**

   Which correction should be made to sentence 3?

   (1) insert a comma after day
   (2) replace should be with has been
   (3) replace undertaken with undertook
   (4) change the spelling of medical to medicle
   (5) no correction is necessary

10. Sentence 5: **The diet drinks are only available through hospital-based programs where all patients' blood pressures, heart rates, and blood chemistries are checked at least twice a month to monitor his health condition.**

Which correction should be made to sentence 5?

(1) change <u>are</u> to <u>is</u>
(2) change <u>patients'</u> to <u>patient's</u>
(3) remove the comma after <u>pressures</u>
(4) replace <u>his</u> with <u>their</u>
(5) insert a comma after <u>his</u>

11. Which revision would improve the effectiveness of the article?

Begin a new paragraph

(1) with sentence 4
(2) with sentence 5
(3) with sentence 6
(4) with sentence 7
(5) with sentence 8

12. Sentence 8: **Problems can include fatigue, dry skin, diarrhea, chills, and muscle cramps.**

Which correction should be made to sentence 8?

(1) replace <u>can include</u> with <u>includes</u>
(2) insert a comma after <u>include</u>
(3) remove the comma after <u>fatigue</u>
(4) remove the comma after <u>dry skin</u>
(5) no correction is necessary

13. Sentence 9: **All of these side affects are reversible once the patient starts eating again.**

Which correction should be made to sentence 9?

(1) replace <u>these</u> with <u>them</u>
(2) replace <u>affects</u> with <u>effects</u>
(3) change <u>are</u> to <u>is</u>
(4) insert a comma after <u>reversible</u>
(5) no correction is necessary

14. Sentence 10: **After the fast, most programs encourage dieters for at least a year to enter a maintenance phase.**

The most effective revision of sentence 10 would include which group of words?

(1) After at least a year,
(2) are encouraging a maintenance phase
(3) maintenance phase for at least a year
(4) are encouraging dieters
(5) After a yearly maintenance phase,

15. Sentence 12: **To be admitted to a <u>program a person</u> generally has to be at least 40 pounds overweight.**

Which is the best way to write the underlined portion of this sentence? If the original is the best way, choose option (1).

(1) program a person
(2) program. A person
(3) program, but a person
(4) program, a person
(5) program, although a person

16. Sentence 13: **It is crucial that individuals who are interested in a fasting diet check with there physician prior to beginning a program.**

Which correction should be made to sentence 13?

(1) insert a comma after <u>crucial</u>
(2) insert a comma after <u>diet</u>
(3) replace <u>there</u> with <u>their</u>
(4) insert a comma after <u>physician</u>
(5) no correction is necessary

Renata Myers
3706 Pinedale
Los Angeles, CA 90042

Customer Service Department
Toys Unlimited
43 Fremont Avenue
Los Angeles, CA 90029

Dear Sir or Madam:

(A)

(1) I am writing this letter to commend one of your employees who truly made my day when I were shopping in your store one day last week. (2) This salesperson, Alberta Johnson went above and beyond the call of duty to help your customers in what was a very stressful situation.

(B)

(3) Your store had advertised a sale on all action figures. (4) You would have thought it was the day before christmas, considering the number of people who came to take advantage of this offer. (5) Most of them had brought along their children, too. (6) Children can be a real nuisance when you are shopping. (7) I live in San Francisco. (8) I was visiting my sister in Los Angeles, and I wanted to buy an action figure for her son, my nephew.

(C)

((9) The problems began when the action figures that people wanted were sold out. (10) Tempers began to rise, people getting angry, and there were a lot of crying children. (11) Some of the customers even began to push and shoving each other. (12) That is when your employee, Alberta Johnson, came out and took the time to speak to each one of us individually. (13) She gave lollipops to the children and helped the parents find other toys. (14) Her calm voice and manner had everyone smiling and thanking her by the end.

(D)

(15) You have an invaluable employee in the person of Ms. Alberta Johnson. (16) It is so rare that one finds the kind of poise and patients that she exhibited. (17) I want to thank her again.

Yours truly,
Renata Myers

---

17. Sentence 1: **I am writing this letter to commend one of your employees who truly made my day when I were shopping in your store one day last week.**

    Which is the best way to write the underlined portion of this sentence? If the original is the best way, choose option (1).

    (1) I were
    (2) I was
    (3) I been
    (4) I have been
    (5) I would have been

18. Sentence 2: **This salesperson, Alberta Johnson went above and beyond the call of duty to help your customers in what was a very stressful situation.**

    Which correction should be made to sentence 2?

    (1) change salesperson to salespeople
    (2) insert a comma after Johnson
    (3) insert a comma after beyond
    (4) change your to you're
    (5) no correction is necessary

19. Sentence 4: **You would have thought it was the day before christmas, considering the number of people who came to take advantage of this offer.**

Which correction should be made to sentence 4?

(1) remove have
(2) change was to were
(3) change christmas to Christmas
(4) change came to come
(5) no correction is necessary

20. Which revision would improve the effectiveness of paragraph B?

(1) move sentence 4 to follow sentence 6
(2) remove sentence 5
(3) remove sentence 6
(4) move sentence 3 to follow sentence 7
(5) move sentence 6 to follow sentence 7

21. Sentences 7 and 8: **I live in San Francisco. I was visiting my sister in Los Angeles, and I wanted to buy an action figure for her son, my nephew.**

The most effective combination of sentences 7 and 8 would include which group of words?

(1) San Francisco, but I was
(2) San Francisco, while I was
(3) San Francisco, so I was
(4) San Francisco, and I was
(5) San Francisco, when I was

22. Sentence 10: **Tempers began to rise, people getting angry, and there were a lot of crying children.**

Which is the best way to write the underlined portion of this sentence? If the original is the best way, choose option (1).

(1) people getting
(2) people are getting
(3) people was getting
(4) people were getting
(5) people gotten

23. Sentence 11: **Some of the customers even began to push and shoving each other.**

The most effective revision of sentence 11 would include which group of words?

(1) began to pushing
(2) begun to push
(3) began pushing and shoving
(4) began pushing and to shove
(5) began to push and shoved

24. Which revision would improve the effectiveness of this letter?

Begin a new paragraph

(1) with sentence 10
(2) with sentence 11
(3) with sentence 12
(4) with sentence 13
(5) with sentence 14

25. Sentence 16: **It is so rare that one finds the kind of poise and patients that she exhibited.**

Which correction should be made to sentence16?

(1) replace one with I
(2) insert a comma after poise
(3) replace patients with patience
(4) insert a comma after patients
(5) replace she with they

Jackson County Agricultural Extension Service

How to Plan a Vegetable Garden

(A)

(1) Many people who grow vegetable gardens to increase the quality of the produce their families consume. (2) Other reasons people are attracted to backyard gardening. (3) These reasons include the convenience of having fresh vegetables close at hand and the savings accrued by growing their own food.

(B)

(4) When planning your vegetable garden, the vegetables you choose to grow should be the ones your family likes the best and eat most often. (5) It's also important to find an appropriate place to plant your vegetables. (6) Contrary to popular belief, it do not take much space to grow a few vegetables. (7) Even if you live in an apartment, you can grow most of your own fresh produce in tubs or window gardens. (8) After the initial soil preparation and planting, gardens only need weekly weeding and watering in order to thrive until the plants are ready to be harvested. (9) Some plants such as tomatoes, peppers, squash, and cucumbers will continue to produce the entire Summer. (10) Other plants such as peas, radishes, green beans, and corn will produce a large harvest only within one or two weeks during the season.

(C)

(11) In planning your garden, it's important to think ahead about what you will do with the extra produce that is harvested during this short time span. (12) Surplus vegetables can be frozen or put into cans to provide low-cost food year-round from the garden.

26. Sentence 1: **Many people who grow vegetable gardens to increase the quality of the produce their families consume.**

    Which correction should be made to sentence 1?

    (1) remove who
    (2) insert a comma after gardens
    (3) change increase to increases
    (4) change consume to consumes
    (5) no correction is necessary

27. Sentences 2 and 3: **Other reasons people are attracted to backyard gardening. These reasons include the convenience of having fresh vegetables close at hand and the savings accrued by growing their own food.**

    The most effective combination of sentences 2 and 3 would include which group of words?

    (1) reasons do not include
    (2) vegetables include
    (3) gardening is that the
    (4) gardening include the
    (5) therefore, it includes

28. Sentence 4: **When planning your vegetable garden, the vegetables you choose to grow should be the ones your family likes the best and eat most often.**

Which is the best way to write the underlined portion of this sentence? If the original is the best way, choose option (1).

(1) eat
(2) eats
(3) ate
(4) has eaten
(5) would have eaten

29. Sentence 6: **Contrary to popular belief, it do not take much space to grow a few vegetables.**

Which is the best way to write the underlined portion of this sentence? If the original is the best way, choose option (1).

(1) do not take
(2) will not take
(3) does not take
(4) has not taken
(5) have not taken

30. Sentence 7: **Even if you live in an apartment, you can grow most of your own fresh produce in tubs or window gardens.**

Which correction should be made to sentence 7?

(1) replace grow with have grown
(2) insert a comma after grow
(3) replace your with his or her
(4) insert a comma after produce
(5) no correction is necessary

31. Which revision would improve the effectiveness of this article?

Begin a new paragraph

(1) with sentence 6
(2) with sentence 7
(3) with sentence 8
(4) with sentence 9
(5) with sentence 10

32. Sentence 9: **Some plants such as tomatoes, peppers, squash, and cucumbers will continue to produce the entire Summer.**

Which correction should be made to sentence 9?

(1) remove the comma after peppers
(2) change continue to continues
(3) insert a comma after produce
(4) change Summer to summer
(5) no correction is necessary

33. Sentence 10: **Other plants such as peas, radishes, green beans, and corn will produce a large harvest only within one or two weeks during the season.**

Which is the best way to write the underlined portion of this sentence? If the original is the best way, choose option (1).

(1) will produce a large harvest only
(2) will only produce a large harvest
(3) produces the largest harvest only
(4) produced a large harvest only
(5) will produce a large only harvest

34. Sentence 11: **In planning your garden, it's important to think ahead about what you will do with the extra produce that is harvested during this short time span.**

Which correction should be made to sentence 11?

(1) change it's to its
(2) insert a comma after ahead
(3) change is to are
(4) insert a comma after harvested
(5) no correction is necessary

35. Sentence 12. **Surplus vegetables can be frozen or put into cans to provide low-cost food year-round from the garden.**

Which is the best way to write the underlined portion of this sentence? If the original is the best way, choose option (1).

(1) or put into cans
(2) or be put into cans
(3) or canned
(4) or tried to be canned
(5) or will be put into cans

MEMORANDUM

TO: All Employees
FROM: J. Mosley, Human Resources
RE: Computer System Upgrade: Departmental Training

(A)

(1) As you all know, Morton Billing Systems will be introducing an upgraded computer system into all departments this will happen soon over about the next six weeks. (2) This will affect all employees who work with computers.

(B)

(3) We will hold training sessions that will very from department to department. (4) You will receive a schedule showing the dates for your department's two-week training period, during which time your new computer systems be installed and you will receive group training. (5) In addition, a team of trainers will spend a week in each department to answer questions and dealing with any problems that might arise during the start-up period. (6) Once the systems are running smoothly, a service hotline will be only a phone call away.

(C)

(7) We think the benefits of the new system would be evident to all. (8) The new system streamlines many data entry processes. (9) In addition, the graphics are upgraded. (10) The new screens are user-friendly. (11) Also, we're getting new lights! (12) We are confident that with your help, the transition process will run smoothly. (13) Working together, we can make this a pleasant experience for all of you.

---

36. Sentence 1: **As you all know, Morton Billing Systems will be introducing an upgraded computer system into all departments this will happen soon over about the next six weeks.**

    The most effective revision of sentence 1 would include which group of words?

    (1) departments over the next six weeks.
    (2) soon introduce
    (3) soon over the next six weeks.
    (4) system soon
    (5) happen in six weeks.

37. Sentence 3: **We will hold training sessions that will very from department to department.**

    Which correction should be made to sentence 3?

    (1) insert <u>most likely</u> before <u>hold</u>
    (2) replace <u>very</u> with <u>vary</u>
    (3) replace <u>that</u> with <u>which</u>
    (4) insert a comma before <u>that</u>
    (5) no correction is necessary

38. Sentence 4: **You will receive a schedule showing the dates for your department's two-week training period, during which time your new computer systems be installed and you will receive group training.**

Which is the best way to write the underlined portion of this sentence? If the original is the best way, choose option (1).

(1) systems be installed
(2) systems will be installed
(3) systems are installed
(4) systems are installing
(5) systems installing

39. Sentence 5: **In addition, a team of trainers will spend a week in each department to answer questions and dealing with any problems that might arise during the start-up period.**

Which is the best way to write the underlined portion of this sentence? If the original is the best way, choose option (1).

(1) to answer questions and dealing
(2) to answering questions and dealing
(3) answering questions and to deal
(4) to answer questions and deal with
(5) to answer questions. And to deal

40. Sentence 7: **We think the benefits of the new system would be evident to all.**

Which is the best way to write the underlined portion of this sentence? If the original is the best way, choose option (1).

(1) would be
(2) will be
(3) being
(4) will have been
(5) would have been

41. Sentences 9 and 10: **In addition, the graphics are upgraded. The new screens are user-friendly.**

The most effective combination of sentences 9 and 10 would include which group of words?

(1) upgraded, the new screens
(2) upgraded the new screens
(3) upgraded, and the new screens
(4) upgraded, but the new screens
(5) upgraded when the new screens

42. Sentence 13. **Working together, we can make this a pleasant experience for all of you.**

Which is the best way to write the underlined portion of this sentence? If the original is the best way, choose option (1).

(1) you
(2) us
(3) them
(4) we
(5) everyone

43. Which revision would improve the effectiveness of paragraph C?

(1) move sentence 7 to follow sentence 8
(2) remove sentence 8
(3) remove sentence 9
(4) remove sentence 10
(5) remove sentence 11

44. Which revision would improve the effectiveness of this memorandum?

Begin a new paragraph

(1) with sentence 8
(2) with sentence 9
(3) with sentence 10
(4) with sentence 11
(5) with sentence 12

BETTER BUSINESS AGENCY
Consumer Information Division

Hiring a Contractor

(A)
(1) Communication between a homeowner and a contractor is important when home improvement projects were planned. (2) Each year, billions of dollars are wasted on home repairs that are not done to a homeowner's satisfaction. (3) To save yourself this kind of headache, follow these steps to hire a reliable contractor.

(B)
(4) The Council of Better Business Bureaus suggests that a homeowner choose a bonded, licensed, or insured contractor. (5) To protect yourself, verify the credentials of the contractor. (6) And talk with some of the contractor's previous customers.

(C)
(7) The terms of agreement should be specified in a written contract. (8) The contract should give complete financial information and specifying the quality and type of materials to be used. (9) Contracts also usually include any warranties on the work performed or the materials used. (10) The start and finish dates for construction should also be included in the contract. (11) Always take time to think over a contract before signing. (12) This is a way to avoid high-pressure sales tactics.

(D)
(13) You should never pay the contractor in cash, and avoid paying the full amount before the work begins. (14) Instead, negotiate a payment plan with the contractor. (15) Inspect the contractor's work and negotiate any disagreements before making a final payment.

(E)
(16) Hiring a reputable contractor will ensure that the remodeling project is done to your satisfaction. (17) Following these guidelines will help protect you and your home.

45. Sentence 1: **Communication between a homeowner and a contractor is important** <u>**when home improvement projects were planned.**</u>

Which is the best way to write the underlined portion of this sentence? If the original is the best way, choose option (1).

(1) when home improvement projects were planned.
(2) if you have planned home improvement projects.
(3) when planning home improvement projects.
(4) because of planning home improvement projects.
(5) although home improvement projects will be planned.

46. Sentences 5 and 6: **To protect yourself, verify the credentials of the contractor. And talk with some of the contractor's previous customers.**

The most effective combination of sentences 5 and 6 would include which group of words?

(1) contractor. And talk
(2) contractor and, talk
(3) contractor and talk
(4) contractor, and, talk
(5) contractor, and talk

47. Sentence 8: **The contract should give complete financial** <u>**information and specifying**</u> **the quality and type of materials to be used.**

Which is the best way to write the underlined portion of this sentence? If the original is the best way, choose option (1).

(1) information and specifying
(2) information, however specifying
(3) information although to specify
(4) information; but specifying
(5) information and specify

48. Sentence 9: **Contracts also usually include any warranties on the work performed or the materials used.**

If you rewrote sentence 9 beginning with

<u>Any warranties on the work performed or the materials used</u>

the next words should be

(1) are usually included
(2) is included
(3) has included
(4) was included
(5) has been usually included

49. Sentences 11 and 12: **Always take time to think over a contract before signing. This is a way to avoid high-pressure sales tactics.**

The most effective combination of sentences 11 and 12 would include which group of words?

(1) Tactics to avoid
(2) To avoid contract signing
(3) Taking time to think over
(4) signing, unfortunately
(5) When high-pressure sales tactics are avoided

50. Sentence 15: **Inspect the contractor's work and negotiate any disagreements before making a final payment.**

Which correction should be made to sentence 15?

(1) change <u>Inspect</u> to <u>Inspecting</u>
(2) change <u>contractor's</u> to <u>contractors</u>
(3) insert a comma after <u>negotiate</u>
(4) insert a comma after <u>disagreements</u>
(5) no correction is necessary

LANGUAGE ARTS, WRITING, Part II

Essay Directions and Topic

Look at the box on the next page. In the box are your assigned topic and the letter of that topic.

You must write on the assigned topic ONLY.

You will have 45 minutes to write on your assigned essay topic. You may return to the multiple-choice section after you complete your essay if you have time remaining in this test period. Do not return the Language Arts, Writing Test until you finish both Parts I and II.

Two evaluators will score your essay according to its overall effectiveness. Their evaluation will be based on the following features:

- Well-focused main points

- Clear organization

- Specific development of your ideas

- Control of sentence structure, punctuation, grammar, word choice, and spelling

REMEMBER, YOU MUST COMPLETE BOTH THE MULTIPLE-CHOICE QUESTIONS (PART I) AND THE ESSAY (PART II) TO RECEIVE A SCORE ON THE LANGUAGE ARTS, WRITING TEST. To avoid having to repeat both parts of the test, be sure to do the following:

- Do not leave the pages blank.

- Write legibly <u>in ink</u> so that the evaluators will be able to read your writing.

- Write on the assigned topic. If you write on a topic other than the one assigned, you will not receive a score for the Language Arts, Writing Test.

- Write your essay on separate lined paper.

TOPIC A

Should the sale of handguns be banned?

In your essay, state your opinion on this issue and use specific examples to support your argument.

Part II is a test to determine how well you can use written language to explain your ideas.

In preparing your essay, you should take the following steps:

- Read the **DIRECTIONS** and the **TOPIC** carefully.
- Plan your essay before your write. Use scratch paper to make any notes. These notes will be collected but not scored.
- Before you turn in your essay, reread what you have written and make any changes that will improve your essay.

Your essay should be long enough to develop the topic adequately.

Adapted with permission of the American Council on Education.

Language Arts, Writing

Part I

The chart below will help you determine your strengths and weaknesses in sentence structure, usage, organization, and mechanics.

Directions: Circle the number of each item that you answered correctly on the Simulated GED Test A. Count the number of items you answered correctly in each column. Write the amount in the Total Correct space of each column. (For example, if you answered 15 Sentence Structure items correctly, place the number 15 in the blank before out of 15). Complete this process for the remaining columns.

Count the number of items you answered correctly in each row. Write that amount in the Total Correct space of each row. (For example, in the Correction row, write the number correct in the blank before out of 24). Complete this process for the remaining rows.

Content / Item Type	Sentence Structure (Unit 1)	Organization (Unit 2)	Usage (Unit 3)	Mechanics (Unit 4)	Total Correct
Correction	26	5, 11, 20, 24, 31, 43, 44	6, 10, 17, 30, 50	2, 7, 12, 13, 16, 18, 19, 25, 32, 34, 37	_____ out of 24
Revision	4, 8, 33, 35, 39, 47		3, 22, 28, 29, 38, 40, 42, 45	15	_____ out of 15
Construction Shift	14, 21, 23, 27, 36, 41, 46, 49		1, 48	9	_____ out of 11
Total Correct	_____ out of 15	_____ out of 7	_____ out of 15	_____ out of 13	Total Correct: _____ out of 50 1–40 = You need more review. 41–50 = Congratulations! You're ready.

If you answered fewer than 41 of the 50 items correctly, determine which areas are hardest for you. Go back to the *Steck-Vaughn GED Writing Skills* book and review the content in those specific areas.

In the parentheses under the heading, the unit numbers tell you where you can find the beginning of specific instruction about that content area in the *Steck-Vaughn GED Writing Skills* book. Also refer to the chart on page 3.

Part II

Directions: Have your instructor or another person read and score your essay. Essays are scored on a scale of 1 to 4, with 1 the lowest score and 4 the highest score. Follow the instructions on page 109.

Enter the reader's score here _____

Ask the reader to help you determine the strong points of the essay and areas where the essay needs improvement. The feedback you receive from the reader will help you improve the next essay you write.

Have your teacher evaluate your essays if you are taking a class. If you are working independently, ask a friend or relative to read your essays. If this is not possible, evaluate your writing yourself. After finishing an essay, put it aside for a day. Then read it as objectively as possible. No matter who checks your writing, make sure that person uses the Essay Scoring Guide on page 109.

LANGUAGE ARTS, WRITING, Part I

Directions

The Language Arts, Writing Simulated Test B is intended to measure your ability to use clear and effective English. It is a test of English as it should be written, not as it might be spoken.

This test consists of paragraphs with numbered sentences. Some of the sentences contain errors in sentence structure, organization, usage, or mechanics (spelling, punctuation, and capitalization). After reading the numbered sentences, answer the multiple choice questions that follow. Some questions refer to sentences that are correct as written. The best answer for these questions is the one that leaves the sentence as originally written. The best answer for some questions is the one that produces a sentence that is consistent with the verb tense and point of view used throughout the paragraph.

You should spend no more than 75 minutes answering the 50 questions on this test. Work carefully, but do not spend too much time on any one question. Do not skip any items. Make a reasonable guess when you are not sure of an answer. You will not be penalized for incorrect answers.

When time is up, mark the last item you finished. This will tell you whether you can finish the real GED Test in the time allowed. Then complete the test.

Record your answers to the questions on a copy of the answer sheet on page 110. Be sure that all required information is properly recorded on the answer sheet.

To record your answers, fill in the numbered space on the answer sheet that corresponds to the answer you choose for each question on the test.

Example:

Sentence 1: **We were all honored to meet governor Phillips.**

What correction should be made to sentence 1?

(1) change <u>honored</u> to <u>honoring</u>
(2) insert a comma after <u>honored</u>
(3) change <u>meet</u> to <u>met</u>
(4) change <u>governor</u> to <u>Governor</u>

(5) no correction is necessary   ① ② ③ ● ⑤

In this example, the word <u>governor</u> should be capitalized; therefore, answer space 4 would be

---

Do not rest the point of your pencil on the answer sheet while you are considering your answer. Make no stray or unnecessary marks. If you change an answer, erase your first mark completely. Mark only one answer space for each question; multiple answers will be scored as incorrect. Do not fold or crease your answer sheet.

When you finish the test, use the Analysis of Performance Chart on page 92 to determine whether you are ready to take the real GED Test and, if not, which skill areas need additional review.

Directions: Choose the <u>one best answer</u> to each question.

Questions 1 through 8 refer to the following article.

How to Make a Child's Trip to the Emergency Room Less Stressful

(A)

(1) Each year the staffs of hospital emergency rooms treats more than 25 million children who are in distress. (2) The most common reasons children are taken to hospitals are trauma (an injury or accident), infectious disease (such as the flu), or a chronic illness (such as asthma).

(B)

(3) Whenever a child is taken to the hospital the experience can be as frightening for the parent as for the child. (4) It is important to try to remain calm in order to make appropriate decisions regarding your child's care. (5) Often hospitals encourage them to stay with their children to provide emotional support.

(C)

(6) Until you are anxious, you need to focus on the child's need to be reassured. (7) Kids take cues from their parents on how to react to situations. (8) If you're hysterical, your child may become more frightened from your reaction than from his or her actual discomfort.

(D)

(9) Try not to contribute to your child's fear. (10) Talk to your child in a soft voice, and explain that what is happening to them will soon be over. (11) You're participation will help the hospital staff treat your child quickly and safely. (12) No parent wants to think of his orher children becoming sick or injured, but when they are, a parent can be the most helpful by remaining calm.

1. Sentence 1: **Each year the staffs of hospital emergency rooms treats more than 25 million children who are in distress.**

   Which correction should be made to sentence 1?

   (1) change <u>rooms</u> to <u>room</u>
   (2) change <u>treats</u> to <u>treat</u>
   (3) insert a comma after <u>treats</u>
   (4) change <u>children</u> to <u>children's</u>
   (5) change <u>who</u> to <u>whom</u>

2. Sentence 2: **The most common reasons children are taken to hospitals are trauma (an injury or accident), infectious disease (such as the flu), or a chronic illness (such as asthma).**

   Which correction should be made to sentence 2?

   (1) change <u>most</u> to <u>more</u>
   (2) insert a comma after <u>children</u>
   (3) change <u>hospitals</u> to <u>hospital's</u>
   (4) remove the comma after <u>accident</u>
   (5) no correction is necessary

3. Sentence 3: **Whenever a child is taken to the hospital the experience can be as frightening for the parent as for the child.**

Which is the best way to write the underlined portion of this sentence? If the original is the best way, choose option (1).

(1) the hospital the
(2) the hospital, the
(3) the hospital, even though
(4) the hospital until
(5) the hospital if

4. Sentence 5: **Often hospitals encourage them to stay with their children to provide emotional support.**

What correction should be made to sentence 5?

(1) insert a comma after Often
(2) change encourage to encourages
(3) replace them with parents
(4) insert a comma after children
(5) no correction is necessary

5. Sentence 6: **Until you are anxious, you need to focus on the child's need to be reassured.**

Which is the best way to write the underlined portion of this sentence? If the original is the best way, choose option (1).

(1) Until you are anxious, you
(2) Although you are anxious, you
(3) Being anxious, you
(4) Overcoming anxiousness, you
(5) If you are anxious, you

6. Sentence 10: **Talk to your child in a soft voice, and explain that what is happening to them will soon be over.**

What correction should be made to sentence 10?

(1) replace in with by
(2) insert a period after voice
(3) change is to are
(4) replace them with him or her
(5) no correction is necessary

7. Sentence 11: **You're participation will help the hospital staff treat your child quickly and safely.**

Which correction should be made to sentence 11?

(1) replace You're with Your
(2) insert a comma after staff
(3) change treat to treats
(4) change quickly to quicker
(5) change safely to safer

8. Sentence 12: **No parent wants to think of his or her children becoming sick or injured, but when they are, a parent can be the most helpful by remaining calm.**

Which is the best way to write the underlined portion of this sentence? If the original is the best way, choose option (1).

(1) injured, but
(2) be injured, but
(3) having been injured, but
(4) injured, unless
(5) injured and unless

How to Barbecue Like a Pro

(A)

(1) Barbecued foods are becoming increasingly popular. (2) Whether it is in the back yard, at the beach, or on an apartment balcony. (3) Barbecuing is an easy way to prepare food. (4) In addition to the traditional steaks, hamburgers, and chicken, cooks are putting fish, vegetables, and cooking breads on a grill. (5) Do your barbecuing secrets begin and end with barbecue sauce? (6) Here are a few tips for jazzing up your barbecuing repertoire, impressing your friends and family, and making some great-tasting food. (7) The wonderful smoky barbecue flavor can be enhanced by adding different kinds of wood. (8) Before adding wood chunks or chips, soak it in water for at least twenty minutes. (9) Then toss the wood onto the hot fire just minutes before placing food on the grill. (10) Other barbecue fanatics throw in grapevines and herbs that lend subtle flavors to grilled food. (11) Most barbecue grills have hot spots, so its best to trim all excess fat from meats. (12) There will be less flareup and smoke if meats is well-trimmed. (13) Vegetables and breads be grilled over lower heat.

(B)

(14) Making an entire meal on a barbecue grill is a cooking method that has been used for centuries. (15) Once a necessity, barbecuing is today a part of a leisure lifestyle that many people enjoy.

9. Sentences 2 and 3: **Whether it is in the back yard, at the beach, or on an apartment balcony. Barbecuing is an easy way to prepare food.**

   The most effective combination of sentences 2 and 3 would include which group of words?

   (1) on an apartment balcony barbecuing
   (2) on an apartment balcony, barbecuing
   (3) on an apartment balcony, and barbecuing
   (4) on an apartment balcony because barbecuing
   (5) on an apartment balcony, when barbecuing

10. Sentence 4: **In addition to the traditional steaks, hamburgers, and chicken, cooks are putting <u>fish, vegetables, and cooking breads</u> on a grill.**

    Which is the best way to write the underlined portion of this sentence? If the original is the best way, choose option (1).

    (1) fish, vegetables, and cooking breads
    (2) fish, cooking vegetables, and breads
    (3) fish, vegetables, and breads
    (4) fish and also cooking vegetables and breads
    (5) fish, vegetables and having cooked bread

11. Sentence 8: **Before adding wood chunks or chips, soak it in water for at least twenty minutes.**

Which correction should be made to sentence 8?

(1) replace Before with While
(2) remove the comma after chips
(3) replace it with them
(4) insert a comma after water
(5) no correction is necessary

12. Sentence 10: **Other barbecue fanatics throw in grapevines and herbs that lend subtle flavors to grilled food.**

Which is the best way to write the underlined portion of this sentence? If the original is the best way, choose option (1).

(1) grapevines and herbs that lend
(2) grapevines and herbs that lends
(3) grapevines and herbs is lent
(4) grapevines and herbs that is lending
(5) grapevines and herbs that are lending

13. Sentence 11: **Most barbecue grills have hot spots, so its best to trim all excess fat from meats.**

Which correction should be made to sentence 11?

(1) change have to has
(2) replace its with it's
(3) insert a comma after trim
(4) insert a comma after fat
(5) no correction is necessary

14. Sentence 12: **There will be less flareup and smoke if meats is well-trimmed.**

Which is the best way to write the underlined portion of this sentence? If the original is the best way, choose option (1).

(1) smoke if meats is
(2) smoke if meats are
(3) smoke, unless meats is
(4) smoke, unless meats are
(5) smoke and if meats are

15. Sentence 13: **Vegetables and breads be grilled over lower heat.**

Which is the best way to write the underlined portion of this sentence? If the original is the best way, choose option (1).

(1) breads be grilled over
(2) breads, having been grilled over
(3) breads has been grilled over
(4) breads should be grilled over
(5) breads is grilled over

16. Which revision would improve the effectiveness of this article?

Begin a new paragraph

(1) with sentence 3
(2) with sentence 5
(3) with sentence 9
(4) with sentence 10
(5) with sentence 13

A New Way to Pop

(A)

(1) Across the country, popcorn a favorite low-calorie snack. (2) Americans buy over 800 million pounds of unpopped popcorn each year. (3) According to the Popcorn Institute located in Chicago. (4) Now, thanks to American ingenuity a new way to pop popcorn has appeared on the market. (5) Two Brothers from Texas have developed a new variety of popcorn. (6) Called "popcorn-on-the-cob," it having been changing the way people think about making popcorn. (7) Here's how it works. (8) When an ear of popcorn are placed in a microwave oven, the kernels burst into the familiar white, crunchy snack. (9) But they stay attached to the cob, providing individual servings. (10) People enjoy watching the popcorn appear before your eyes. (11) The popcorn-on-the-cob snack has captivated kids wherever it's been available, mainly in the Southwest.

(B)

(12) Not satisfied to rest on the success of their invention, the brothers are now looking for ways to improve the new product. (13) There are a lot of new kinds of popcorn popping machines on the market, too. (14) They are currently experimenting with blue, purple, and red popcorn cobs. (15) An offbeat option to the traditional varieties, microwave popcorn-on-the-cob is popping up in grocery stores, gift shops, and mail-order catalogs.

17. Sentence 1: **Across the country, popcorn a favorite low-calorie snack.**

    Which correction should be made to sentence 1?

    (1) remove the comma after country
    (2) insert is after popcorn
    (3) insert were after popcorn
    (4) add a comma after favorite
    (5) no correction is necessary

18. Sentences 2 and 3: **Americans buy over 800 million pounds of unpopped popcorn each year. According to the Popcorn Institute located in Chicago.**

    The most effective combination of sentences 2 and 3 would include which group of words?

    (1) in Chicago, Americans buy
    (2) year; according
    (3) Americans in Chicago
    (4) pounds, according
    (5) year, however the Popcorn

19. Sentence 4: **Now, thanks to American ingenuity a new way to pop popcorn has appeared on the market.**

The most effective revision of sentence 4 would include which group of words?

(1) ingenuity and a new
(2) to pop popcorn, has
(3) popcorn will have been appearing
(4) ingenuity, a new way to pop
(5) thanking to American

20. Sentence 5: **Two Brothers from Texas have developed a new variety of popcorn.**

Which correction should be made to sentence 5?

(1) change Brothers to brothers
(2) insert a comma after Brothers
(3) change have to has
(4) insert a comma after variety
(5) no correction is necessary

21. Sentence 6: **Called "popcorn-on-the-cob," it having been changing the way people think about making popcorn.**

Which is the best way to write the underlined portion of this sentence? If the original is the best way, choose option (1).

(1) having been changing
(2) have been changing
(3) has been changing
(4) have changing
(5) had to have changing

22. Sentence 8: **When an ear of popcorn are placed in a microwave oven, the kernels burst into the familiar white, crunchy snack.**

Which correction should be made to sentence 8?

(1) change are to is
(2) remove the comma after oven
(3) change burst to bursted
(4) insert a comma after familliar
(5) remove the comma after white

23. Sentence 10: **People enjoy watching the popcorn appear before your eyes.**

The most effective revision of sentence 10 would include which group of words?

(1) People enjoys
(2) People enjoy to watch
(3) appear before his or her eyes
(4) appear before them eyes
(5) appear before their eyes

24. Which revision would improve the effectiveness of this article?

Begin a new paragraph

(1) with sentence 5
(2) with sentence 6
(3) with sentence 9
(4) with sentence 10
(5) with sentence 11

25. Which revision would improve the effectiveness of paragraph B?

(1) move sentence 12 to the end of the paragraph
(2) move sentence 13 to the beginning of the paragraph
(3) remove sentence 13
(4) remove sentence 14
(5) remove sentence 15

Questions 26 through 33 refer to the following memorandum.

Wordwide ⊕ Technology

MEMORANDUM

TO: All Employees
FROM: Alice Morgan, Employee Benefits
RE: UPAC Health Fair

(A)

(1) All personal are invited to attend our annual Health Fair. (2) It will be held in the employee cafeteria the week of May 14–18, between the hours of 8 A.M. and 4:30 P.M. (3) Everyone are invited to take time out to check up on his or her health.

(B)

(4) Without knowing it, many people suffer from high blood pressure. (5) Let one of the professionals from our UPAC Health Services test your blood pressure and talking to you about ways to reduce stress. (6) Other experts will be there to speak to people with high levels of cholesterol. (7) Cholesterol is a significant factor in heart disease. (8) Almost 70 percent of the American population suffers from high cholesterol. (9) Studies have shown that cholesterol levels can be reduced 15 to 25 percent through diet modification. (10) Talk to a UPAC dietician about how to modify your diet.

(C)

(11) You can also stop by to test your heart and respiration rates. You can get a free eye checkup, or test your hearing. (12) Smokers can learn how to stop smoking. (13) Women can sign up for free breast cancer screening. (14) In addition, the Red Cross will have a booth at our fair so that you can give blood. (15) We hope this year's turnout topped last year's for this important week. (16) All together we can make this a great event. (17) We look forward to seeing you there!

26. Sentence 1: **All personal are invited to attend our annual Health Fair.**

Which correction should be made to sentence 1?

(1) replace All with Some
(2) insert please before invited
(3) change annual to annually
(4) replace personal with personnel
(5) replace personal with personally

27. Sentence 3: **Everyone are invited to take time out to check up on his or her health.**

Which is the best way to write the underlined portion of this sentence? If the original is the best way, choose option (1).

(1) Everyone are invited
(2) Everyone are being invited
(3) Everyone is invited
(4) You is invited
(5) You have been being invited

28. Which sentence below would be most effective at the beginning of paragraph B?

    (1) Here are some of the ways you can check up on your health at the fair.
    (2) The fair was a huge success last year.
    (3) When was the last time you had a checkup?
    (4) The American Medical Association suggests you visit your family physician twice a year.
    (5) Many employees have been asking about signing up for aerobics and yoga classes.

29. Sentence 5: **Let one of the professionals from our UPAC Health Services test your blood pressure and talking to you about ways to reduce stress.**

    The most effective revision of sentence 5 would include which group of words?

    (1) Letting one of the professionals
    (2) testing your blood pressure and talking
    (3) test your blood pressure and talk to you
    (4) ways to reducing stress and live
    (5) reduce stress and living longer

30. Sentences 6 and 7: **Other experts will be there to speak to people with high levels of cholesterol. Cholesterol is a significant factor in heart disease.**

    The most effective combination of sentences 6 and 7 would include which group of words?

    (1) cholesterol it is a
    (2) cholesterol, it is a
    (3) cholesterol being a
    (4) cholesterol, considered by many to be
    (5) cholesterol a significant

31. Sentence 15: **We hope this year's turnout topped last year's for this important week.**

    The most effective revision of sentence 15 would include which group of words?

    (1) We will hope
    (2) We hoped
    (3) turnout will top
    (4) turnout has topped
    (5) turnout be topping

32. Sentence 16: **All together we can make this a great event.**

    Which correction should be made to sentence 16?

    (1) replace All together with Altogether
    (2) replace can with could
    (3) move all together to follow this
    (4) replace great with greater
    (5) no correction is necessary

33. Which revision would improve the effectiveness of this memorandum?

    Begin a new paragraph

    (1) with sentence 12
    (2) with sentence 13
    (3) with sentence 14
    (4) with sentence 15
    (5) with sentence 16

Questions 34 through 42 refer to the following letter.

Alonzo Rodriguez
1423 River Drive
Atlanta, GA 30384

Mr. Martin Paulsen, Hiring Officer
Board of Education
Richmond, VA 23217

Dear Mr. Paulsen:

(A)

(1) I am writing in response to the advertisement I saw in the Sunday newspaper for the position of peer counciling administrator. (2) I am interested in this position, I am enclosing my resume for your consideration.

(B)

(3) Let me tell you a little about myself I have been a high school gym teacher for three years. (4) I have run programs in conflict resolution and conducted training sessions for both teachers and students. (5) In addition, I started a conflict resolution training program for parents, which was quiet successful. (6) I think conflict resolution is very important. (7) I also worked to develop a community outreach program for our school. (8) Many of this school's families are from other countries, they are not familiar with the American education system. (9) To help families such as these I ran workshops on how to help children do homework. (10) I also ran a workshop on how to apply to college.

(C)

(11) In addition to my experience, I have excellent recommendations from the principle of my school as well as from other administrators.

(D)

(12) I will contacts you within a few days to confirm receipt of my resume. (13) Thank you for your time.

Sincerely,
Alonzo Rodriguez

---

34. Sentence 1: **I am writing in response to the advertisement I saw in the Sunday newspaper for the position of peer counciling administrator.**

    Which correction should be made to sentence 1?

    (1) change writing to write
    (2) replace response with respond
    (3) change Sunday to sunday
    (4) replace peer with pier
    (5) replace counciling with counseling

35. Sentence 2: **I am interested in this position, I am enclosing my resume for your consideration.**

    Which is the best way to write the underlined portion of this sentence? If the original is the best way, choose option (1).

    (1) position, I
    (2) position I
    (3) position and am
    (4) position because I
    (5) position while I

36. Sentence 3: **Let me tell you a little about myself I have been a high school gym teacher for three years.**

    Which is the best way to write the underlined portion of this sentence? If the original is the best way, choose option (1).

    (1) myself I
    (2) myself and I
    (3) myself, I
    (4) myself because I
    (5) myself. I

37. Sentence 5: **In addition, I started a conflict resolution training program for parents, which was quiet successful.**

    Which correction should be made to sentence 5?

    (1) remove In addition,
    (2) insert also after I
    (3) insert a comma after training
    (4) remove the comma after parents
    (5) replace quiet with quite

38. Sentence 8: **Many of this school's families are from other countries, they are not familiar with the American education system.**

    Which is the best way to write the underlined portion of this sentence? If the original is the best way, choose option (1).

    (1) other countries, they
    (2) other countries they
    (3) other countries. They
    (4) other countries because they
    (5) other countries when they

39. Sentence 9: **To help families such as these I ran workshops on how to help children do homework.**

    Which is the best way to write the underlined portion of this sentence? If the original is the best way, choose option (1).

    (1) such as these I
    (2) such as these, I
    (3) such as these. I
    (4) such as these so I
    (5) such as these then I

40. Which revision would improve the effectiveness of paragraph B?

    (1) remove sentence 3
    (2) move sentence 3 to follow sentence 9
    (3) remove sentence 6
    (4) move sentence 8 to follow sentence 9
    (5) remove sentence 9

41. Sentence 11: **In addition to my experience, I have excellent recommendations from the principle of my school as well as from other administrators.**

    Which correction should be made to sentence 11?

    (1) replace as well as with in addition to
    (2) insert a comma after recommendations
    (3) replace principle with principal
    (4) insert a comma after school
    (5) insert a comma after as

42. Sentence 12: **I will contacts you within a few days to confirm receipt of my resume.**

    Which is the best way to write the underlined portion of this sentence? If the original is the best way, choose option (1).

    (1) I will contacts
    (2) I be contacting
    (3) I will contact
    (4) I am contacting
    (5) I are contact

Stress and You

(A)

(1) The stress of modern life was taking an immense toll on your health. (2) Current estimates are that 80% of the visits to Doctors in America are for stress-related diseases. (3) While stress itself is not necessarily hazardous to your health, your reaction to stress can affect your body. (4) When you're under stress, good eating habits are often ignored. (5) You deplete your body of essential nutrients. (6) Stress also makes your body secrete additional hormones which speed up their bodily functions.

(B)

(7) Scientists are convinced that relaxation is the key to coping with stress. (8) When you're relaxed, your heart and rate of breathing slow down. (9) Blood pressure declines. (10) By learning how to relax for just ten minutes a day, you can lower your stress level and more energy can be had. (11) You can control your stress instead of allowing your stress to control you. (12) There are many different ways of relaxing. (13) Some people find that vigorous exercising relaxes them. (14) Others prefer more meditative practices such as yoga or tai chi. (15) What works for you.

43. Sentence 1: **The stress of modern life was taking an immense toll on your health.**

    Which is the best way to write the underlined portion of this sentence? If the original is the best way, choose option (1).

    (1) life was taking
    (2) life have been taking
    (3) life may be taking
    (4) life were taking
    (5) life has been taking

44. Sentence 2: **Current estimates are that 80% of the visits to Doctors in America are for stress-related diseases.**

    Which correction should be made to sentence 2?

    (1) insert a comma after are
    (2) insert a comma after visits
    (3) change Doctors to doctors
    (4) change America to america
    (5) replace for with because

45. Sentences 4 and 5: **When you're under stress, good eating habits are often ignored. You deplete your body of essential nutrients.**

    The most effective combination of sentences 4 and 5 would include which group of words?

    (1) stress habits are
    (2) ignored, and your body is
    (3) essential nutrients that
    (4) ignored, but you
    (5) your body under stress

46. Sentence 6: **Stress also makes your body secrete additional hormones which speed up their bodily functions.**

    The most effective revision of sentence 6 would include which group of words?

    (1) makes the body
    (2) your body, secrete
    (3) additionally hormones
    (4) up your bodily
    (5) Stress functions

47. Sentence 8: **When you're relaxed, your heart <u>and rate of breathing</u> slow down.**

Which is the best way to write the underlined portion of this sentence? If the original is the best way, choose option (1)

(1) and rate of breathing
(2) rate and breathing rate
(3) and to breathe more slowly
(4) rate and breathing more slowly
(5) and slow breathing rate

48. Sentence 10: **By learning how to relax for just ten minutes a day, you can lower your stress level and <u>more energy can be had.</u>**

Which is the best way to write the underlined portion of this sentence? If the original is the best way, choose option (1).

(1) more energy can be had.
(2) having more energy.
(3) to have more energy.
(4) feel more energetic.
(5) feeling more energy.

49. Which revision would improve the effectiveness of this article?

Begin a new paragraph

(1) with sentence 9
(2) with sentence 10
(3) with sentence 11
(4) with sentence 12
(5) with sentence 13

50. Sentence 15: **What works for you.**

The most effective revision of sentence 15 would include which group of words?

(1) It's important to find
(2) and what doesn't
(3) and how much you can do
(4) What works for some people
(5) Some people say

LANGUAGE ARTS, WRITING, Part II

Essay Directions and Topic

Look at the box on the next page. In the box are your assigned topic and the letter of that topic.

You must write on the assigned topic ONLY.

You will have 45 minutes to write on your assigned essay topic. You may return to the multiple-choice section after you complete your essay if you have time remaining in this test period. Do not return the Language Arts, Writing Test until you finish both Parts I and II.

Two evaluators will score your essay according to its overall effectiveness. Their evaluation will be based on the following features:

- Well-focused main points
- Clear organization
- Specific development of your ideas
- Control of sentence structure, punctuation, grammar, word choice, and spelling

REMEMBER, YOU MUST COMPLETE BOTH THE MULTIPLE-CHOICE QUESTIONS (PART I) AND THE ESSAY (PART II) TO RECEIVE A SCORE ON THE LANGUAGE ARTS, WRITING TEST. To avoid having to repeat both parts of the test, be sure to do the following:

- Do not leave the pages blank.
- Write legibly <u>in ink</u> so that the evaluators will be able to read your writing.
- Write on the assigned topic. If you write on a topic other than the one assigned, you will not receive a score for the Language Arts, Writing Test.
- Write your essay on separate lined paper.

Adapted with permission of the American Council on Education.

TOPIC B

Compare and contrast the experience of children who have a parent care for them at home with the experience of children who are cared for at day-care centers during work hours.

In your essay, be specific and give examples to support your comparison.

Part II is a test to determine how well you can use written language to explain your ideas.

In preparing your essay, you should take the following steps:

- Read the **DIRECTIONS** and the **TOPIC** carefully.
- Plan your essay before you write. Use scratch paper to make any notes. These notes will be collected but not scored.
- Before you turn in your essay, reread what you have written and make any changes that will improve your essay.

Your essay should be long enough to develop the topic adequately.

Language Arts, Writing

Part I

The chart below will help you determine your strengths and weaknesses in sentence structure, usage, organization, and mechanics.

Directions: Circle the number of each item that you answered correctly on the Simulated GED Test B. Count the number of items you answered correctly in each column. Write the amount in the Total Correct space of each column. (For example, if you answered 15 Sentence Structure items correctly, place the number 15 in the blank before out of 15). Complete this process for the remaining columns.

Count the number of items you answered correctly in each row. Write that amount in the Total Correct space of each row. (For example, in the Correction row, write the number correct in the blank before out of 24). Complete this process for the remaining rows.

Content / Item Type	Sentence Structure (Unit 1)	Organization (Unit 2)	Usage (Unit 3)	Mechanics (Unit 4)	Total Correct
Correction	2, 17	16, 24, 25, 28 33, 40, 49	1, 4, 6, 11, 22 23	7, 13, 20, 26 32, 34, 41, 44	_____ out of 24
Revision	5, 10, 35, 36 38, 45, 47, 48		12, 14, 15, 21, 27, 42, 43	3, 8, 19, 39	_____ out of 19
Construction Shift	9, 18, 29, 30 50		31, 46		_____ out of 7
Total Correct	_____ out of 15	_____ out of 7	_____ out of 15	_____ out of 13	Total Correct: _____ out of 50 1–40 = You need more review. 41–50 = Congratulations! You're ready.

If you answered fewer than 41 of the 50 items correctly, determine which areas are hardest for you. Go back to the *Steck-Vaughn GED Writing Skills* book and review the content in those specific areas.

In the parentheses under the heading, the unit numbers tell you where you can find the beginning of specific instruction about that area of grammar in the *Steck-Vaughn GED Writing Skills* book. Also refer to the chart on page 3.

Part II

Directions: Have your instructor or another person read and score your essay. Essays are scored on a scale of 1 to 4, with 1 the lowest score and 4 the highest score. Follow the instructions on page 109.

Enter the reader's score here _____

Ask the reader to help you determine the strong points of the essay and areas where the essay needs improvement. The feedback you receive from the reader will help you improve the next essay you write.

Have your teacher evaluate your essays if you are taking a class. If you are working independently, ask a friend or relative to read your essays. If this is not possible, evaluate your writing yourself. After finishing an essay, put it aside for a day. Then read it as objectively as possible. No matter who checks your writing, make sure that person uses the chart on this page as a guide.

UNIT 1: Sentence Structure

Sentence Fragments
Page 4

Sentences will vary. Following are examples of correct sentences.

1. Adults in the class are learning about how to make their own car repairs.
2. S
3. The labor union council will meet to decide what sites to picket.
4. The person was charged with drunken driving after falling asleep at a traffic light.
5. Mr. Contreras, the only resident who is against the plan, did not attend.
6. She plans to buy the deluxe vacuum cleaner since it is on sale.
7. S
8. A survey of twenty-two cities that are considering new property taxes was conducted.
9. S
10. A contract was issued to repair over half of the state's crumbling bridges.
11. After deciding to go to the lake and buy the necessary fishing permits, we began our trip.
12. The low-income housing project will be located near Huntley Park.
13. S
14. S
15. Educators plan to boycott the reduction of funds for the community college library's computer system.
16. S
17. Most of the drug-related deaths reported in 2000 were caused by cocaine.
18. On the way to the local discount store, I saw a video store's offer of three movies for $5.00.
19. S
20. The school committee member argued that "children have the right to know how to protect themselves."
21. S
22. When the polls have closed and all the votes have finally been counted, the candidate will know if she is the new state senator.

Run-On Sentences
Page 5

Answers will vary. Following are examples of correct paragraphs.

Paragraph 1:

People who have been divorced know that the breakup of a marriage can leave deep scars on their children. Children often think they are at fault for the divorce. They blame themselves for being "bad" children. Children are also afraid that they will become latchkey kids. Sometimes they fear that they will become homeless or have to live in a shelter. They may have fantasies about the absent parent returning. Some become victims of custody battles and have to choose between their mother and father.

Paragraph 2:

The credit card industry is less than forty years old. Some credit cards have offered real convenience. Those accepting credit cards include hospitals for open-heart surgery and the federal government for income taxes. Credit cards have made debt the American way of life. Instead of saving for a washer and dryer, some people merely charge them. They do not realize that it may cost them more to charge than to pay cash. As a result of easy access to credit, many American families are over their heads in debt.

Comma Splices
Page 6

Sentences will vary. Following are examples of correct sentences.

1. Janet decided to cook spaghetti, so she filled a pot with water and put it on the stove.
2. Lucas walked home slowly. He was daydreaming.
3. Several students raised their hands. They knew the answer to the question.
4. S
5. The artists were hanging their work in the gallery. The opening was that night.
6. Every college student needs a computer. Some students lease them.
7. S
8. She rearranged her room because she wanted a better work environment.
9. S
10. S
11. We bought her a lovely vase for her birthday because she loves flowers.
12. S
13. My grandmother called last night. We all spoke with her.
14. There were four messages on his answering machine. One of them was urgent.
15. S
16. I have to get back to my studying, so wake me up in one hour.
17. My little brother hates to be teased, and my little sister loves to tease him.
18. The company decided to file for bankruptcy. It seemed to be the only way out.
19. S
20. S
21. S
22. S
23. S
24. S

Identifying and Correcting Fragments, Run-Ons, and Comma Splices
Page 7

Answers will vary. Following are examples of correct paragraphs.

Last week, our current school principal, Janet Malcolm, announced she will not be returning to her post next year. She has decided to take a year's leave to stay home with her baby. A special committee has been created to begin the search to find someone to fill her post.

The Search Committee met on Monday for the first time. It consists of two staff members (Bob Matthews and myself) and two parent representatives (Joan Anzalone and Lee Brick). Joan and Bob agreed to draft the job notice.

Candidates for the position will be interviewed by the Search Committee. Candidates will be submitting portfolios and visiting some of our classrooms. They are also expected to meet with the staff for an informal question-and-answer session.

We want to wish Janet the very best. We will keep you informed of the Search Committee's progress in the coming weeks, because we want to assure you of our commitment to keeping Park Elementary School a school of quality.

Sentence Combining
Page 8

Answers may vary. Following are examples of correct answers.

1. , or
2. , but
3. , but
4. , or
5. , so
6. , or
7. , and
8. , but
9. , and
10. , yet *or* and
11. , but
12. , but
13. , nor
14. , but
15. , so
16. , or
17. , yet

Sentence Combining II
Page 9

Sentences will vary. Following are examples of correct sentences.

1. Advanced Business System's training program was very costly, but their record of job placement was excellent.
2. Although she often gets tired of the paperwork, the police officer is very efficient.
3. Last week he bought on sale a new set of carpet mats for the car.
4. Most brands of lunchmeat contain artificial preservatives that are used to retard spoilage.
5. We can leave for the restaurant as soon as I make these phone calls.
6. While I finish washing the windows, could you please mow the lawn?
7. Some companies use drug testing as a standard part of their pre-employment process.
8. Even though grocery stores in the inner city and the suburbs are often run by the same company, prices for the same product are often different.
9. "Happy Days Are Here Again" was one of the most well-known, popular songs of the 1930s.
10. The package addressed to her grandchild was mailed on Wednesday by Mrs. Sinata.
11. The report, recently filed by the Internal Investigation Unit, caused controversy within the agency.
12. My appointment was scheduled for the morning, but it was noon before I saw the doctor.
13. The Disney-MGM Studios Theme Park, near Orlando, Florida, cost $500 million to build.
14. General Motors' Corvette ZR1 has a top speed of 180 m.p.h. and can go from 0 to 60 m.p.h. in 4.2 seconds.
15. Although scientists R. Stanley Pons and Martin Fleischmann claimed they found a simpler way to generate fusion, many other scientists said that their work was flawed.
16. I had nightmares for ten years after I had a car accident at sixteen.
17. Child safety seats have become important devices because they reduce injury to children in car accidents.
18. It will stop raining soon, and then we can go for a walk or to the park.
19. A VCR allows viewers to tape TV shows to be watched at a more convenient time.

Subordination
Page 10

Sentences will vary. Following are examples of correct sentences.

1. Mr. Johnson has to leave early in order to pick up his son from the day-care center.
2. Since the hurricane had destroyed the mobile home park, the federal government provided emergency assistance.
3. Newspapers can give specific details of a story, while television news usually only reports the general outline.
4. Tooth decay has decreased significantly, probably because toothpaste now contains flouride.
5. Because the quality of future life depends on us, the Environmental Protection Agency wants to act now to protect the environment.
6. Even if we could save enough money for the down payment, we would still need to have money for moving costs and initial repairs.

7. When I take Mother to visit her friends, I will stop at the cleaners and drop off the clothes.

8. The new findings show that dairy products contain fat as well as calcium and vitamins.

9. Although I would like to go with you, I have to care for my sister's children while she's in the hospital.

10. Unless the problem of drug use is addressed, many of our children will become victims.

11. Since I don't get home from work until after 6:00, I miss seeing the 5:30 TV news shows every day.

12. Because my dental hygienist is gentle and does not cause me discomfort when she cleans my teeth, I plan to continue getting my teeth cleaned every six months.

13. After I save money from my paycheck this month, I will be able to buy a new CD player.

14. The band has been playing much better recently because they have been practicing a lot and learning new material.

Subordination II
Page 11

1. b	5. b	9. b	13. b
2. a	6. b	10. b	14. a
3. a	7. a	11. a	15. a
4. a	8. b	12. a	16. a

Parallel Structure
Page 12

1. The residents volunteered to board up abandoned buildings, wash graffiti off the walls, and patrol the park.

2. The employees were asked to stock the shelves, take inventory, and sweep the floor.

3. Beginning the preparations now will be better than postponing them.

4. To prevent crime, both police protection and community involvement are necessary.

5. Mr. Cutter thinks travel is exciting because it allows him an opportunity to meet new people and to see different places.

6. The hospital staff asked the patient for his name, address, and phone number.

7. People tend to exercise more regularly if they do more than one activity; for example, a person could alternate bicycling, walking, and swimming.

8. It's quiet now because Josh is sleeping, Trina is playing outside, and Brian is reading a book.

9. On the weekends we enjoy going out to eat, shopping in the malls, and driving in the country.

10. Many fast-food restaurants' milkshakes are not made with milk but with fillers, flavorings, and added chemicals.

11. When examining a house, always check for water marks on the walls, water pressure in the faucets, and sediment in the pipes.

12. A small family business has a better chance of being profitable if its product is unique, uses common ingredients, and has fairly low prices.

13. To live well requires a belief in one's self, an attitude of fairness, and a desire to help others.

14. Using fertilizer, watering regularly, and weeding every week can improve the harvest from your garden.

15. The Bill of Rights guarantees our freedom of speech, our right to assemble peacefully, and our right to bear arms.

16. Neither exercising nor eating less food is the best way to lose weight; the best way is to combine the two.

17. Reading good books, watching movies, and playing softball are three of my favorite hobbies.

18. At noon I'll deposit my paycheck, put gas in the car, and buy some bread.

19. Painting pictures and playing music are two ways for individuals to express their creativity.

20. The special dinner at China Palace comes with egg rolls, fried rice, and wonton soup.

Misplaced Modifiers
Page 13
Answers will vary. Following are examples of correct sentences.

1. My neighbor bought the used car with low mileage from a reputable dealer.

2. During lunch the plant supervisor discussed the possibility of implementing the employee medical coverage plan.

3. In the boss's office, we discussed plans for the annual company picnic.

4. I returned the defective lawn mower that I had bought to the store.

5. The chef's assistant mixed the ingredients for the cake filling in the blender.

6. The janitor located the missing file behind the secretary's desk.

7. Mr. Meyers yelled angrily at the children who were playing in the street.

8. The sentence is correct as written.

9. The caseworker with the beautiful long hair was explaining the application procedure to a client in the lobby.

10. Jorge looked sadly at the newly purchased car destroyed by the fallen tree.

11. Mrs. Cheng found the missing lottery tickets stuffed in the drawer.

12. We waved to the smiling boy coming up the driveway on a skateboard.

13. Jennifer was cleaning out the file cabinet containing over fifty-four software disks.

14. The painter, wearing overalls, began work on the rented house.

15. The Mississippi River, which is over two miles wide, has been polluted by factory waste.

16. The keys to the computer room were covered by the papers on the desk, so we couldn't locate them.

17. Mrs. Kaspar was waiting impatiently for her physician to call with the test results.

18. The sentence is correct as written.

19. The police officers caught the bank manager, who had been embezzling funds for years, disposing of the incriminating evidence.

20. Elwin purchased a compact disc player with seven special features from the audio store.

21. Manufacturers are trying to produce a cigarette made of herbs for smokers.

22. Holding his golf clubs, Richard fed the cat.

23. Have you ever been bitten by fire ants when you were working in the garden?

24. Coming up on your left is the American Mutual Life building.

Dangling Modifiers
Page 14
Sentences will vary. Following are examples of correct sentences.

1. While I was enjoying lunch with my co-workers, my car was stolen.

2. While the ambulance was going to the hospital, it was hit by a car.

3. The sentence is correct as written.

4. When I was thirteen, my family moved back East.

5. While I was walking home from the bus stop, my umbrella was caught by the wind and blew away.

6. The sentence is correct as written.

7. While I was waiting for the check to arrive in the mail, the bills became overdue.

8. After I had worked all day, the bed was a welcome sight.

9. While rushing to get to work, I was delayed by a flat tire on the car.

10. The sentence is correct as written.

11. When I was parking at the mall, my car was hit by a man who wasn't paying attention to what he was doing.

12. As they were wondering what to do next, the supervisors stopped the assembly line and discussed the problem.

13. Exhausted and sunburned, I was glad my trip would soon come to an end.

14. The sentence is correct as written.

15. As we were walking through the discount store, we saw that the aisles were cluttered with merchandise.

16. The real estate agent showed us the big, old, worn-out house.

17. After I read the recipe, I baked a casserole for the guests.

18. While I was speaking to a group of strangers, my knees knocked and my hands shook.

19. Before he booked the thief, the police officer advised him of his right to consult a lawyer.

20. While I was walking in the park, a huge dog bit my leg.

21. While Pat was reeling in the line quickly, the fish jumped off the hook.

22. After we searched around the office, we found the contract on a chair.

23. The excited boy reeled in his first fish, which was dangling from the fishhook in its mouth.

24. Jack watched the vultures as they circled overhead.

25. It started to rain while I was walking the dog around the block.

26. While Henry and Lynn were cleaning out the attic, they found an old family photograph album.

27. Their friends took them to an expensive, fancy new restaurant.

Sentence Revising
Page 15
Sentences will vary. Following are examples of correct sentences.

1. Because the mayor was under pressure, he had to act quickly.

2. Brett went to the Department of Public Safety office in order to take the driver's license examination.

3. The woman who provided the information which led to the conviction was given the reward money.

4. We didn't have any hot water because the electricity that runs the water heater has been off since the storm.

5. If I take enough time to assemble the ingredients, the recipe will be easy to prepare.

Sentence Revising II
Page 16
Sentences will vary. Following are examples of correct sentences.

1. While swimming has traditionally been a popular recreational activity, concern about safety keeps thousands of swimmers off the beaches.

2. Because cellular telephones can be used for business, home, and leisure, they are becoming widely popular.

3. The largest amusement park in America, Cedar Point, is located in Sandusky, Ohio.

4. If fifteen lifeguards are not hired by May 30, Little Rock won't be able to open its municipal pools.

5. The fire marshal reported that an increase in destructive, fatal fires in Idaho shows the public indifference to safety.

6. Since the drummer in the rock band has taken a regular job, he won't be available.

GED Practice: Sentence Structure
Page 17–19

1. **(4) he has started** The rewritten sentence is, "Because Jerome is determined to stop drinking, he has started going to Alcoholics Anonymous meetings."

2. **(3) adults** The rewritten sentence is, "By calling the AIDS national hotline, adults can get free written information."

3. **(1) Although he may never have seen a Porsche, he's** The rewritten sentence is, "Although he may never have seen a Porsche, he's probably heard about that car."

4. **(5) Rick** The rewritten sentence is, "Before he turned on the VCR to watch the movie he had rented, Rick threw the empty pizza boxes on the floor."

5. **(4) All the kids gather at** The rewritten sentence is, "All the kids gather at the neighborhood recreation center, which has adults supervising the children at all times."

6. **(3) are** The rewritten sentence is, "The individuals who go to the park to enjoy the sights and sounds of nature are angered by the many people who take boom boxes."

7. **(3) The Irish Setters he owned** The combined sentence reads, "The Irish Setters he owned were his constant companions."

8. **(2) Because Jessie** The combined sentence reads, "Because Jessie is the best cook in the family, everyone says she should open a restaurant."

9. **(3) Although penicillin** The combined sentence reads, "Although penicillin is a commonly used antibiotic, there are some people who have a severe allergy to it."

10. **(1) immediately, and it** The combined sentence reads, "The corner store has items that people need immediately, and it is convenient because it is close to home."

11. **(2) small, and** The combined sentence reads, "The community was very small, and it had one radio station that played only Big Band music from the 1930s."

12. **(2) Since she had** The combined sentence reads, "Since she had been feeling ill for the last two hours, the secretary decided to go home early."

13. **(3) coffee because I** Option (3) corrects the sentence fragment. Options (2) and (5) use inappropriate connecting words. Option (4) inserts an unnecessary comma.

14. **(5) friends, and she** Only option (5) corrects the comma splice by creating a compound sentence with the connecting word *and*.

15. **(2) When you're shopping at the grocery store,** Option (2) corrects the dangling modifier by adding the object to which it refers (you). Option (3) does not correct the dangling modifier. Option (4) uses an inappropriate pronoun (he), and option (5) uses an inappropriate subordinating word (because).

16. **(5) friendly. They** Option (5) corrects the run-on sentence by creating two separate sentences. Option (2) creates a comma splice. Options (3) and (4) insert inappropriate connecting words.

17. **(2) much, I** Option (2) uses a comma to connect the fragment to the sentence. Options (3), (4), and (5) add connecting words that do not make sense.

18. **(3) early. You** Option (3) corrects the comma splice by creating two separate sentences. Option (2) creates a run-on sentence. Options (4) and (5) insert inappropriate connecting words.

UNIT 2: Organization

Topic Sentence
Page 20
1. b
2. a
3. c
4. a
5. b
6. b

Supporting Details
Page 21
1. b
2. c
3. c
4. a
5. c
6. a

Unity and Coherence
Page 22
1. a
2. c
3. b
4. c

Unity and Coherence II
Page 23

Paragraph 1: Cross out these sentences: A symbol is something that stands for something else and The picture of a telephone receiver would be recognized anywhere in the world.

Paragraph 2: Cross out these sentences: You must be 18 years of age or older before an election to be eligible to vote. and To vote, you need to be an American citizen and be able to show proof of residence.

Dividing Paragraphs
Page 24
1. For ordinary, run-of-the-mill back pain (not resulting from injury or internal damage), there are some simple exercises anyone can do.

2. The success or failure of a big-budget film can make or break a studio in any given year.

3. The UN performs many different functions in the world.

Dividing Paragraphs II
Page 25

Answers will vary. Following are examples of correct paragraphs.

Paragraph 1:

What is the appeal of horror movies? Some people say that watching a scary movie gives you the same type of thrill you get on a roller coaster as you approach the top and look down. You scream and yell, remaining safe all the while. These horror fans assert that watching horror films is a normal way to relax and let out tension in a basically harmless and entertaining environment. But others argue that horror movies are a perverse part of today's culture that we should really examine.

Horror movies seem to be particularly popular among teenage audiences. In recent years, there have been several new horror films with the requisite sequels. These films often star young Hollywood actors from popular TV shows with established fan bases. Many young people seem to have grown up watching films of this kind. For these die-hard horror fans, the more blood and gore, the better.

Paragraph 2:

The controversy over dress codes in public schools continues. There are two sides to this issue. Some people feel a dress code creates a more serious academic environment. Many parents feel their children give too much attention to their clothes. Other advocates argue that a school uniform helps eliminate divisions within the student body based on money and clothing styles. Proponents of dress codes also say that a school uniform takes the burden of deciding what to wear every day off the student.

On the other hand, many people feel that a dress code violates an individual's freedom of expression. Students enjoy expressing their personality and beliefs through their clothing choices. They say that the dress code issue merely shifts attention away from real academic and social issues that need to be addressed. Improving academic standards, they say, is about better training for teachers and more money for schools.

Dividing Multi-paragraph Documents
Page 26

Not more than fifty years ago, computers were enormous things that filled entire rooms. They were used exclusively by the government, the military, and big business. Today, computers fit comfortably into the palm of your hand, and they are everywhere.

The history of the computer's development is fascinating. As far back as 1623, Wilhelm Schickard, a German professor, built the first-known mechanical calculator. A little more than three hundred years later, the American mathematician Howard Aiken built a 50-foot digital computer which for the first time expressed numbers as digits. In 1971, the Intel 4004 chip was completed, paving the way for the first microprocessor. In 1975, the first desktop microcomputer became available. In 1980, the Microsoft Corporation adapted an operating system for personal computers, which opened up the market to the general public.

Today it is estimated that more than a third of American households have at least one personal computer. This is more than any other country in the world. Meanwhile, innovations in technology are causing us to redefine how, when, and for what we use our computers. We have integrated them into almost every aspect of modern life. They are used in offices to help people find information, compose letters and reports, and keep track of business profits. Computers can be found in toys as well as in high-tech medical equipment and spacecraft.

In the future, high-speed access to information, education, and entertainment systems will allow delivery of services never dreamed of before. For better or worse, computers are here to stay.

Students should recognize that the first paragraph break comes with the shift to the topic of the history of computers. The next break comes when the topic shifts to computers in our lives today. The final break comes when the topic shifts to the future—the conclusion of the text.

Dividing Multi-paragraph Documents II
Page 27

What kinds of parks and open space do we want in our community? This is a timely question, since it was recently announced that state funds have been earmarked for creating more parks in Union County.

Our city council conducted a survey on this very question, and it's an issue about which I am concerned, too. The city council announced the findings of its survey yesterday. The survey results show that people mainly are interested in having more soccer fields and sports facilities. There is nothing wrong with this, at first glance. However, I question whether these survey results accurately reflect the needs of our community.

First, the city council's survey was sent almost exclusively to people who are interested in athletics and sports. It was sent out to team coaches, boy scout clubs, and directors of other recreational programs. Naturally, these are the very people who are looking for more athletic facilities. If the council follows this path, soccer fields are going to pop up everywhere. Every soccer field will have its parking lot. Every parking lot will have its roads. All the cars will spew carbon dioxide and other pollutants.

Second, I am concerned that very little was said about maintaining our current parks. Our largest park, designed by Frederick Law Olmstead (who is mostly known for creating Central Park in New York City), is a real treasure. This park retains most of Olmstead's original design. It was created to give city people a place for quiet contemplation and enjoyment of the outdoors.

Unfortunately, the park's vistas and expansive fields have been seized upon by our city planners as the ideal spaces to become sports fields. I think this is a big mistake. I urge our city council to reconsider its decision before destroying some of our last remaining open spaces.

New paragraphs are needed when a new idea is introduced. Transitions are used to introduce these shifts in topic. The first two transitions are used to show the order of the writer's concerns. The last transition introduces the writer's concluding paragraph.

Dividing Multi-paragraph Documents III
Page 28

The second and third paragraphs should be combined.

The third paragraph continues on the topic of the Nobel Prize. The fifth and sixth paragraphs should also be combined, since the topic for both is entertainment industry awards.

Dividing Multi-paragraph Documents IV
Page 29

Essays will vary but should have paragraphs with clear topic shifts, as well as the use of transitional words or phrases to introduce new ideas.

GED Practice: Organization
Pages 30–33

1. **(4) remove sentence 2** Sentence 2 detracts from the unity of the paragraph. The other changes do not make sense.

2. **(1) insert this sentence after sentence 5: I included proof of my income, proof of residence, and a copy of Ronald's birth certificate and social security card, as required.** Option (1) supplies a detail relevant to the letter. Option (2) supplies a detail that is not relevant. The other options do not make sense.

3. **(3) with sentence 9** Sentence 9 has the transitional phrase Then in January. Options (1), (2), (4), and (5) would result in ineffective text division.

4. **(1) remove sentence 12** This sentence detracts from the unity of the paragraph. The other options do not make sense.

5. **(2) move sentence 14 to come before sentence 13** This logical order makes the most sense.

6. **(5) I am angry about how this matter is being handled.** Options (1), (2), and (3) are inappropriate. Option (4) is too general.

7. **(5) Spring is just around the corner and that means the start of another exciting company softball season.** Option (5) is broad enough to encompass the main idea of the paragraph without being too broad.

8. **(4) First,** Option (4) supplies an effective transition. The other options supply inappropriate transitions.

9. **(2) remove sentence 5** Sentence 5 is a tangent and should be removed.

10. **(1) combine paragraphs B and C** Paragraph C continues the same topic (anyone can play on the team) as Paragraph B.

11. **(4) with sentence 19** Sentence 19 introduces a new topic.

12. **(4) To make it easier** This choice offers a transition that fits the meaning of the sentence.

UNIT 3: Usage

Subject-Verb Agreement
Page 34

1.	has	11.	expect
2.	were	12.	dump
3.	has	13.	is
4.	increases	14.	plan
5.	try	15.	become
6.	has	16.	is
7.	want	17.	avoid
8.	Does	18.	eat
9.	take	19.	are
10.	brings	20.	float

Subject-Verb Agreement II
Page 35

1.	anticipate	12.	expects
2.	was	13.	has
3.	believe	14.	want
4.	play	15.	contain
5.	were	16.	has
6.	was	17.	are
7.	have, need	18.	encourage
8.	have	19.	are
9.	has	20.	need
10.	were, were	21.	has
11.	was	22.	wants

Subject-Verb Agreement III
Page 36

1.	was	9.	checks
2.	C	10.	show
3.	were	11.	has
4.	C	12.	C
5.	relates	13.	say
6.	are	14.	were
7.	C	15.	were
8.	Does		

Regular and Irregular Verbs
Page 37

1.	forgiven	9.	rung
2.	played	10.	reminded
3.	done	11.	known
4.	took	12.	is singing
5.	is listening	13.	warned
6.	begun	14.	fallen
7.	hurt	15.	done
8.	asked	16.	felt

Regular and Irregular Verbs II
Page 38

1.	jogged	9.	shaken
2.	sprayed	10.	forgotten
3.	driven	11.	sang
4.	frozen	12.	given
5.	broken	13.	spoke
6.	bled	14.	finished
7.	drawn	15.	notified
8.	gone	16.	washed

Verb Tenses
Page 39
1. reports
2. will purchase *or* purchase
3. remains *or* had remained
4. warn *or* have warned
5. increased *or* have increased
6. sponsors *or* sponsored
7. refused
8. is requesting
9. is planting *or* has planted
10. is rising *or* has risen

Tense Sequence
Page 40
1. has increased *or* will increase *or* increased
2. will decline *or* will have declined
3. had learned *or* learned
4. punished
5. sent
6. will have
7. ignored
8. had *or* was having
9. has offered
10. will have planted *or* had planted
11. have eaten
12. will decide
13. saw

Pronouns
Page 41
1. his
2. them *or* mine
3. he
4. us
5. we
6. hers
7. its
8. your
9. mine
10. them
11. your
12. theirs
13. them
14. we
15. I, he, *or* she
16. them

Pronoun Antecedents
Page 42
1. his — Mr. Peabody
2. their — cats
3. their — they
4. its — house
5. their — Edward and Allan
6. her — Ms. Gutierrez
7. its — box
8. her — Jennifer nor Maxine
9. it — bag
10. his — Jimmy nor Sam
11. their — people
12. her — Mother Nature
13. their — Americans
14. its — program
15. their — parents

Pronoun Shifts and Ambiguous References
Page 43
Sentences will vary. Following are examples of correct sentences.
1. <u>they</u> Caroline is learning about the stock market because it is going up at the moment.
2. <u>he</u> The student became very nervous when the teacher questioned him.
3. <u>they</u> She lost her job last week because her company was laying people off.
4. <u>him</u> My brother thanked my uncle for his thoughtful gift.
5. <u>her</u> Margaret asked Aiyana, "Does your dress fit?"
6. <u>they</u> We never buy fresh meat at that grocery store because the owners overcharge.
7. <u>it</u> My older brother is a computer technician, but I'm not interested in computer technology.
8. <u>he</u> When Bradley was promoted, he told Simon.
9. <u>it</u> I can't play that new computer game on my monitor because the CD is defective.
10. <u>her</u> Mary called Jacqueline at work to say that Jacqueline's sister had given birth to a baby girl.

GED Practice: Usage
Pages 44–48
1. **(2) change <u>are</u> to <u>is</u>** The singular verb <u>is</u> is needed to match the subject <u>symbol</u>.
2. **(5) no correction is necessary** The sentence is correct as written.
3. **(2) can discover** The past perfect tense is inconsistent with the tense clues in the paragraph. Options (3), (4), and (5) are also inconsistent tenses.
4. **(1) are** <u>Are</u> matches the plural subject (<u>typical fruits</u>) and is in the present tense. Options (2), (3), (4), and (5) supply incorrect subject-verb agreement or inappropriate tense.
5. **(2) is being provided** The continuing present tense is the correct tense for this passage. All the other options put the verb in an inappropriate tense.
6. **(3) change <u>does</u> to <u>do</u>** The plural verb <u>do</u> is needed to match the subject <u>they</u>. The verb <u>are</u> is used correctly. Option (4) creates error in tense and subject-verb agreement.
7. **(2) are beginning to offer** The rest of the passage is in the present tense. Only option (2) is in present tense and also matches the plural subject.
8. **(3) change <u>attract</u> to <u>attracts</u>** <u>Each</u> is a singular subject matched by <u>attracts</u>. The other options make errors in tense or subject-verb agreement.
9. **(1) change <u>offers</u> to <u>offer</u>** <u>Supermarkets</u> is a plural subject matched by <u>offer</u>. The other options make errors in tense or subject-verb agreement or both.
10. **(4) change <u>were</u> to <u>are</u>** The rest of the passage is in the present tense. The verb <u>say</u> is used correctly.

11. **(2) change <u>has</u> to <u>have</u>** The plural subject <u>Americans</u> takes the plural form of the verb <u>have</u>. The other options make errors in subject-verb agreement or in tense.

12. **(2) the children's limited** Only option (2) clarifies the vague pronoun reference.

13. **(2) than there were.** Only option (2) makes sense for tense agreement in this sentence.

14. **(5) change <u>shares</u> to <u>share</u>** The plural verb <u>share</u> matches the subject <u>people</u>.

15. **(3) provides** The singular subject <u>option</u> requires the singular verb <u>provides</u>. The other options are not consistent with the present tense of the passage.

16. **(1) services keep pace** The other options use inappropriate tenses.

17. **(5) no correction is necessary** The sentence is correct as written.

18. **(5) that keep elderly people** <u>Elderly people</u> is needed to clarify who keeps active. None of the other options correct this ambiguous pronoun reference; in addition, the other options create inconsistent use of tense.

19. **(4) There is always** The passage is written in the present tense.

20. **(2) isn't able to cook** Only option (2) has a singular, present tense verb to match the singular subject <u>resident</u>.

21. **(1) Either of these options is** <u>Either</u> is always singular and requires the singular verb <u>is</u>.

22. **(5) no correction is necessary** The sentence is correct as written.

23. **(2) You and they** As part of a compound subject, <u>they</u> is the correct pronoun form. Options (3), (4), and (5) supply incorrect verb tenses.

24. **(4) to shop for books.** The pronoun <u>them</u> has no antecedent. Only option (4) corrects this ambiguous reference.

25. **(5) unzipped version of the book** The antecedent <u>book</u> in the preceding sentence is singular, and warrants repeating to avoid ambiguity. The verb <u>is</u> agrees with the singular subject <u>option</u>. The passage is written in present tense, so options (2) and (3) supply incorrect verb tenses.

26. **(2) PC users need** The plural subject <u>users</u> requires the plural verb <u>need</u>. The verb tenses should remain present to be consistent with the rest of the letter.

27. **(2) If you try** The pronoun <u>you</u> should remain consistent throughout the letter. The tense should remain in the present.

28. **(5) to have bought** The past participle of <u>to bring</u> is <u>brought</u>. <u>Are</u> is in the correct tense.

UNIT 4: Mechanics

Capitalization
Page 49
1. director, state
2. Fourth of July
3. Doctor
4. Japanese, German
5. correct as written
6. Martin Luther King
7. Congress
8. Pacific Ocean
9. Jamaica, tourist
10. high school, Community College
11. correct as written
12. world, Africa
13. spring, unions
14. French, Italian
15. city, utility
16. cousin, biology, history
17. French
18. judge

Comma Use
Page 50
1. The Community Action Center needs volunteers to prepare food, package individual meals, and deliver food to elderly shut-ins.
2. Answering questions regarding nuclear waste, the spokesperson for the electric company was visibly nervous.
3. Anthony Ching, the union's shop steward, provides the company with a list of repairs needed each week to ensure worker safety.
4. The newspaper editor asked the reporter to investigate the accident, determine the real cause, and identify the person responsible for the damage.
5. Until she had completed the probationary period, the new employee was not allowed to use the chemicals alone.
6. To fully understand the situation, the dismayed parents asked to speak to the principal.
7. Patients are taught about sound nutrition, appropriate exercise, and stress reduction.
8. Mrs. Landover, the most active club member, suggested conducting a bowl-a-thon to raise money.
9. After the job was completed, the contractor checked to see if the customers were satisfied.
10. The first things we did after unpacking were make some coffee, put our feet up, and relax.
11. The list containing the names, addresses, and phone numbers of each of the applicants was given to the employment office.
12. Jonathan Welch, a senator from Texas, introduced legislation that would provide stricter punishment for drug pushers.
13. On the way to her job, Ms. Chaney drops off her daughter at the Sunshine Child Care Center.
14. Isaac Asimov, an award-winning scientist, also wrote many books.

15. When spring begins, many Americans prepare their income tax forms for the Internal Revenue Service.

16. Our summer garden is producing corn, squash, tomatoes, cucumbers, and green peppers.

17. Bats, birds, moths, and butterflies help plants to transfer their pollen from the male to the female plants.

18. Agates, semiprecious stones, have bands of different colors.

19. Table salt, a mineral, is found in rocks, soil, and oceans.

20. The sentence is correct as written.

21. Swimming, jogging, walking, and riding bicycles are all good forms of exercise.

Comma Use II
Page 51

1. The vocational component of Dawson Technical Institute offers a program in machine repair.

2. The woman who identified the criminal was given a reward by the prosecutors.

3. The carpet was completely ruined by the flood.

4. To comply with state health regulations, people without shoes are not allowed into most restaurants.

5. Alonzo was watching Monday night football.

6. Erica Roberts, my mother's swimming instructor, finished her certification just last year.

7. The sentence is correct as written.

8. Yesterday the excited bride-to-be bought the invitations, addressed the envelopes, and deposited them in the mail.

9. I voted for the senator four years ago.

10. The driver of the car that went speeding through the red light was stopped immediately by the police.

11. The sentence is correct as written.

12. Sarah Williams was given the Outstanding Adult Student Award for her commitment to helping others further their education.

13. The runner who was determined to win first place concentrated on his breathing.

14. The sentence is correct as written.

15. When planting flowers or vegetables, always water the ground thoroughly.

16. Citizens who want good leaders must get out to vote in local elections.

17. The car with the power windows and power locks is the one I want.

18. The passengers and the crew boarded the airplane slowly.

19. Rollerblading, also called inline skating, became a popular sport during the 1990s.

20. Knowing how to use a computer has become an important job skill.

21. Anna's friends have decided to throw her a surprise birthday party next month.

22. The sentence is correct as written.

23. The man at the next table is talking so loudly that we cannot carry on our own conversation.

24. Benjamin's aunt, uncle, and cousin came to visit him during the holidays.

25. The sentence is correct as written.

26. Did you leave your umbrella and your briefcase on the bus?

27. The sentence is correct as written.

28. Workplace safety rules are designed to protect workers in all kinds of situations.

29. The sentence is correct as written.

30. I'll talk to my supervisor about getting a raise.

Comma Use III
Page 52

1. Mrs. Rashad works full time at the bank, but she also attends Washington Evening School to prepare for her GED examination.

2. The sentence is correct as written.

3. The caseworkers were frustrated and upset, for they had just been informed that the child had run away from home again.

4. I went to this morning's meeting with a lot of misgivings, but it turned out to be a very productive two hours.

5. Doctors urge patients to develop a healthier diet, and they encourage regular exercise to strengthen the heart muscle.

6. My mother thinks I ought to study medicine, but I am more interested in anthropology.

7. There is not a lot of interest in today's seminar, nor is there much interest in the brainstorming session planned for tomorrow.

8. They all wanted to hike to the top of the mountain, but my feet hurt and I just wanted to rest.

9. I have never been scuba diving, but my brother tells me it is a great experience.

10. The sentence is correct as written.

11. The unpopular candidate tried to address the key issues in the campaign, but the angry crowd kept interrupting his speech.

12. The mayor announced this morning that he did not plan to run for senator, but his supporters have urged him to reconsider his decision.

13. My grandmother must leave at 6:00 A.M., or she will miss her flight to Italy.

14. Sebastian is nervous about the kayaking trip, for he is not a very experienced swimmer.

15. Lawanda was enraged when she found out that she had been cheated out of thousands of dollars, and she wrote a blistering letter to the Better Business Bureau.

16. I do not plan to attend the reception, nor can I go to the dinner.

17. The judge called the court to order, but the prosecution was not ready to call its first witness.

18. She knew the prognosis was not good, but she did not give up hope.

19. Brett was proud to receive the grand prize, for he had worked long and hard on his project.

20. The American Heart Association urges middle-aged men to get cholesterol screenings, and it suggests a low-fat diet to lower a high cholesterol level.

21. Marilyn can return to school next semester, or she can look for a job.

22. She has no plans for marriage, nor does she want to have children.

Spelling: Contractions and Possessives
Page 53

1. buyer's
2. suspect's
3. Florida's
4. missiles'
5. correct as written
6. can't, don't
7. couldn't, children's
8. weren't
9. car's, hadn't
10. hadn't, I'd
11. it's
12. Frank's, won't
13. President's
14. Chicago's
15. reporter's
16. family's, wasn't
17. isn't
18. You'll
19. company's
20. didn't, I'll
21. he'd, didn't, I've
22. plan's
23. Hasn't
24. She's
25. You're
26. don't
27. City's
28. correct as written

Spelling: Plural and Possessive Nouns
Page 54

1. mother's
2. rights
3. government's
4. children's
5. Lujan's
6. deer's
7. eye's
8. co-workers'
9. searchers
10. Yesterday's
11. stores'
12. bookcase's
13. passengers
14. children's

Spelling: Homonyms
Page 55

1. bored
2. whole
3. feat
4. passed
5. principal
6. new *or* whole
7. past
8. affect
9. Hear
10. break
11. hole
12. knew
13. principle
14. effect
15. brake
16. accept
17. Here
18. feet

Spelling: Homonyms II
Page 56

1. its
2. who's
3. It's
4. they're
5. there
6. whose
7. your
8. their
9. You're
10. it's
11. your
12. who's
13. their
14. they're
15. there
16. whose
17. they're

GED Practice: Mechanics
Pages 57–60

1. **(1) change Whose to Who's** Who's is a contraction of who is, which is the correct phrasing for a question. No commas are needed.

2. **(3) asleep, and** Two independent clauses joined by a coordinating conjunction must have a comma before the conjunction. Option (2) results in a sentence fragment. Options (4) and (5) use inappropriate conjunctions.

3. **(2) insert a comma after psychological** An interrupting phrase must have commas before and after it. The comma after insomnia is also needed for that reason. No other commas are needed.

4. **(4) include pain, use of** Use a comma to separate items in a list. No other choice has the correct punctuation.

5. **(2) exercising vigorously, avoiding** Use a comma to separate items in a list. No other choice has the correct punctuation.

6. **(5) no correction is necessary** The sentence is correct as written. No commas are needed in this sentence.

7. **(5) no correction is necessary** Pills is a plural noun in this sentence. No commas are needed.

8. **(3) sleep by not allowing** No internal punctuation is needed in this sentence.

9. **(2) change persons to person's** The possessive form is needed to show ownership of the eyes. A comma is needed after an introductory phrase. Movie is not a proper noun. No other commas are needed.

10. **(4) In the past, insomnia** Passed is the past tense of pass. The comma is required after the introductory clause. No capitalization is required.

11. **(2) insert a comma after trees** A comma is needed to set off the interrupting phrase. The comma after Earth is needed for the same reason. The possessive form of California is needed to show ownership of the trees. No other commas are needed.

12. **(3) change america to America** America is a proper noun and must be capitalized. No commas are needed. Vikings must be capitalized because it is a proper noun.

13. **(4) change Million to million** A common noun should not be capitalized. No commas are needed. Redwoods, a plural noun, is the subject of the sentence, not a possessive noun.

14. **(3) remove the comma after along** No internal punctuation is needed.

15. **(5) no correction is necessary** The sentence is correct as written. No internal punctuation is needed. No capitalization is needed.

16. **(3) preserves have, of course, become** The homonym course should replace coarse. The commas are correct in the original sentence.

17. **(1) arrive by bus, but** The sentence is correct as written—two independent clauses joined with a connecting word must have a comma before the conjunction.

18. **(2) Their efforts are rewarded, however,** The possessive pronoun is needed here to speak of the efforts of the tourists. The use of commas is correct in the original sentence.

19. **(1) change parks to park's** The possessive form is needed to show ownership of the terrain. No commas are needed.

20. **(1) insert a comma after particular** A comma is needed to set off the General Sherman Tree , an appositive. No other commas are needed.

21. **(3) replace feat with feet** The tree is measured in feet. The punctuation in the sentence is correct.

22. **(2) replace past with passed** The correct word in the sentence is the past tense of to pass . No additional commas are needed. California should be capitalized.

SIMULATED TEST A

Pages 62–73

1. **(4) change uses to use** (Usage/Subject-Verb Agreement) The subject appliances is plural and requires the plural verb use . In option (1), each would refer to one appliance. Option (2) inserts an unnecessary comma. Option (3) is incorrect because a comma is needed prior to an interrupting phrase.

2. **(1) remove the comma after boards** (Mechanics/Comma Use). Options (2) and (3) are singular verbs and do not agree with the plural subject boards . Option (4) inserts an unnecessary comma.

3. **(2) are manufactured** (Usage/Verb Tenses) The paragraph is in present tense. Options (1) and (4) are in past tense; option (5) is in future tense; and option (3) does not match the plural subject.

4. **(5) overused, the copper** (Sentence Structure/ Fragments) Option (5) connects the dependent clause with the independent clause. Option (2) fails to insert a comma after the dependent clause. Options (3) and (4) do not convey an appropriate relationship.

5. **(5) no revision is necessary** (Organization/Topic Sentence-Coherence) The topic sentence is effective. The other options result in a lack of unity and coherence.

6. **(2) is being tested.** (Usage/Subject-Verb Agreement) The singular verb is matches the singular subject technology . Option (1) is plural. Options (3), (4), and (5) are in the wrong tense.

7. **(4) change scientists to scientists'** (Spelling/ Possessives) The reference is to the creativity of the scientists, so the correct form is the plural possessive scientists' . Option (1) is the wrong tense. Option (2) inserts an unnecessary comma. Option (3) is a singular, not a plural, possessive.

8. **(4) food is eaten, but** (Sentence Structure/ Fragments) A helping verb must be used with the past participle eaten . Options (3) and (5) do not match the present tense of the sentence. Option (2) uses a plural verb instead of the required singular form.

9. **(1) insert a comma after day** (Mechanics/ Comma Use) A comma must be used before and after an interrupting phrase. Option (2) is in the wrong tense. Option (3) cannot be used because helping verbs are present. Option (4) would make the spelling of medical incorrect.

10. **(4) replace his with their** (Usage/Pronouns) The pronoun their agrees in number with the antecedent patients . Option (1) is singular. Option (2) would be used if the sentence involved only one patient. Option (3) is incorrect because commas must be used to separate items in a list. Option (5) inserts a comma where it is not necessary.

11. **(3) with sentence 6** (Organization/Dividing Paragraphs) Sentence 6 is a good topic sentence for a new paragraph about the drawbacks of liquid diets. The other options do not offer reasonable, logical text divisions.

12. **(5) no correction is necessary** (Mechanics/ Commas Use) The sentence is correct as written. Option (1) is incorrect because it does not match the plural subject. Options (2), (3), and (4) incorecctly use commas in a series.

13. **(2) replace affects with effects** (Mechanics/ Homonyms) The correct word is effects . Option (1) replaces a correct pronoun with an incorrect pronoun. Option (3) is incorrect because it does not match the plural subject. Option (4) is incorrect because a comma is not needed when the dependent clause follows the independent one.

14. **(3) maintenance phase for at least a year** (Sentence Structure/Modifiers) Option (3) corrects the misplaced modifier for at least a year . The other options do not correct the misplaced modifier, or they change the meaning of the sentence.

15. **(4) program, a person** (Mechanics/Comma Use) When a dependent clause comes before an independent one, it must be set off with a comma. Option (2) produces a sentence fragment. Options (3) and (5) do not have logical connecting words.

16. **(3) replace there with their** (Mechanics/ Homonyms) The possessive pronoun their must be used to refer to individuals . No commas are needed in this sentence.

17. **(2) I was** (Usage/Subject-Verb Agreement). The correct verb form for the subject I is was . Options (1) and (3) are incorrect usage. Options (4) and (5) are inappropriate verb tenses for this paragraph.

18. **(2) insert a comma after <u>Johnson</u>** (Mechanics/ Comma Use). <u>Alberta Johnson</u> is an appositive that needs to be set off by commas. In Option (1), <u>salespeople</u> is plural, while <u>Johnson</u> is singular. Option (3) inserts an unnecessary comma. Option (4) replaces the correct objective pronoun <u>me</u> with <u>I</u>.

19. **(3) change <u>christmas</u> to <u>Christmas</u>** (Mechanics/ Capitalization). <u>Christmas</u> is a proper noun and must be capitalized. Option (1) replaces the correct verb form <u>would have thought</u> with an incorrect verb form. Option (2) replaces the correct singular form of subject-verb agreement with an incorrect plural. Option (4) replaces the correct verb tense <u>came</u> with <u>come</u>.

20. **(3) remove sentence 6** (Organization/Unity and Coherence). Effective paragraph coherence is achieved by removing this tangent. Options (1), (2), (4), and (5) create incoherence.

21. **(1) San Francisco, but I was** (Sentence Structure/Subordination). The connecting word <u>but</u> improves the clarity of the relationship between the two sentences. Options (2), (3), and (5) present connecting words that confuse the relationship between the two sentences. Option (4) presents the connecting word <u>and</u> which creates repetition.

22. **(4) people were getting** (Usage/Verb Tenses). <u>Were</u> is the correct auxiliary verb for the plural noun <u>people</u>. Option (2) presents an inappropriate present progressive tense form. Options (3) and (5) present incorrect verb forms.

23. **(3) began pushing and shoving** (Sentence Structure/Parallel Structure). Option (3) corrects the faulty parallelism in the sentence. Option (1) creates an incorrect verb form <u>began to pushing</u>. Option (2) adds the incorrect verb tense <u>begun</u>. Options (4) and (5) do not correct the faulty parallelism.

24. **(3) with sentence 12** (Organization/Dividing Paragraphs). This creates a paragraph focusing attention on the commendable behavior of the employee who is the subject of the letter. All the other options create inappropriate paragraph divisions.

25. **(3) replace <u>patients</u> with <u>patience</u>** (Mechanics/Homonyms). Only option (3) corrects the confusion of the homonyms <u>patients</u> and <u>patience</u>. Option (1) does not agree with the verb <u>finds</u>. Options (2) and (4) insert unnecessary commas. Option (5) changes a correct pronoun to an incorrect one.

26. **(1) remove <u>who</u>** (Sentence Structure/Fragments) By removing <u>who</u>, the original sentence fragment becomes a complete sentence: "Many people grow vegetable gardens to increase the quality of produce their families consume." Option (2) inserts an incorrect comma. Options (3) and (4) would result in a singular verb with the plural subject <u>families</u>.

27. **(4) gardening include the** (Sentence Structure/ Subordination) The combined sentence is: "Other reasons people are attracted to backyard gardening include the convenience of having fresh vegetables close at hand and the savings accrued by growing their own food." The other choices do not make logical connections.

28. **(2) eats** (Usage/Subject-Verb Agreement) The singular verb <u>eats</u> matches the singular subject <u>family</u>. Options (3), (4), and (5) are the wrong tense.

29. **(3) does not take** (Usage/Verb Tenses) Only option (3) is singular to match the subject and is in the present tense. Options (2), (4), and (5) are the wrong tense.

30. **(5) no correction is necessary** (Usage/Pronouns) The sentence is correct as written.

31. **(3) with sentence 8** (Organization/Dividing Paragraphs) This creates a new paragraph on the harvest schedules of different vegetables. None of the other choices results in an effective text division.

32. **(4) change <u>Summer</u> to <u>summer</u>** (Mechanics/ Capitalization) The names of the seasons are not capitalized. Option (1) removes a comma necessary for items in a series. Option (2) replaces the correct verb form with an incorrect form, and option (3) adds an unnecessary comma.

33. **(2) will only produce a large harvest** (Sentence Structure/Modifiers) The adverb <u>only</u> should be placed as close to the verb phrase as possible to make the meaning of this sentence clear.

34. **(5) no correction is necessary** (Mechanics/ Comma Use) The sentence is correct as written.

35. **(3) or canned** (Sentence Structure/Parallel Structure) Only Option (3) is in parallel structure with the verb <u>frozen</u>.

36. **(1) departments over the next six weeks.** (Sentence Structure/Run-ons) This is the only choice that effectively corrects the run-on sentence and maintains the coherence of the sentence.

37. **(2) replace <u>very</u> with <u>vary</u>** (Mechanics/ Homonyms). Only Option (2) provides the correct choice between the homonyms <u>very</u> and <u>vary</u>.

38. **(2) systems will be installed** (Usage/Verb Tenses). Option (2) uses the correct verb form and tense consistent with the text. Options (3), (4), and (5) create incorrect verb forms.

39. **(4) to answer questions and deal with** (Sentence Structure/Parallel Structure). Options (2) and (3) do not correct the faulty parallelism in the sentence. Option (5) creates a sentence fragment.

40. **(2) will be** (Usage/Verb Tenses). Option (2) is the only choice with a verb tense consistent with the rest of the text.

41. **(3) upgraded, and the new screens** (Sentence Structure/Sentence Combining). Option (3) adds a connecting word and a comma to create a compound sentence. Option (2) creates a run-on sentence. Options (4) and (5) use connecting words that do not make sense.

42. **(2) us** (Usage/Pronouns) Option (2) correctly uses us to refer back to we. None of the other options is correct.

43. **(5) remove sentence 11** (Organization/Unity and Coherence) Sentence 11 is a tangent that detracts from the unity of the paragraph. The other options create incoherence.

44. **(5) with sentence 12** (Organization/Dividing Paragraphs) Option (5) results in a new paragraph that focuses on closing comments. The other options do not make sense for the beginning of a new paragraph.

45. **(3) when planning home improvement projects.** (Usage/Verb Tenses) Options (1) and (2) are not in the present tense. Options (4) and (5) do not have logical connecting words. Only option (3) makes sense in this sentence.

46. **(3) contractor and talk** (Sentence Structure/ Fragments) Option (3) corrects the sentence fragment. Option (1) does not correct the sentence fragment and also introduces a comma error. Options (2), (4), and (5) incorrectly separate the compound verbs verify and talk with a comma.

47. **(5) information and specify** (Sentence Structure/ Parallel Structure) Option (5) corrects the faulty parallelism in the sentence. Options (1), (2), (3), and (4) do not have verb forms in parallel structure with the verb give.

48. **(1) are usually included** (Usage/Subject-Verb Agreement) The rewritten sentence is: "Any warranties on the work performed or materials used are usually included in the contract." All other options contain singular verb forms that do not match the plural subject warranties.

49. **(3) Taking time to think over** (Sentence Structure/Subordination) The rewritten sentence is: "Taking time to think over a contract before signing it is a way to avoid high-pressure sales tactics." The other word groups do not make sense.

50. **(5) no correction is necessary** (Usage/Verb Tenses) This sentence is correct as written.

SIMULATED TEST B

Pages 78-89

1. **(2) change treats to treat** (Usage/Subject-Verb Agreement). The plural verb treat matches the plural subject staffs. No comma is needed. Rooms, children, and who are used correctly.

2. **(5) no correction is necessary** (Sentence Structure/Parallel Structure) The sentence is correct as written.

3. **(2) the hospital, the** (Mechanics/Comma Use) When a dependent clause comes before an independent clause, use a comma. Options (3), (4), and (5) do not use logical connecting words.

4. **(3) replace them with parents** (Usage/ Pronouns) Parents makes the meaning of the pronoun clear. Commas are not needed after often or children. The plural form of the verb encourage matches the plural subject hospitals, so it does not need to be changed.

5. **(2) Although you are anxious, you** (Sentence Structure/Subordination) Only the word although indicates the proper relationship between the two clauses.

6. **(4) replace them with him or her** (Usage/ Pronouns) Them is a plural pronoun that incorrectly refers to a singular antecedent child. Option (1) and (3) create errors. The period in Option (2) is unnecessary

7. **(1) replace You're with Your** (Mechanics/ Possessives & Contractions) Your is a possessive pronoun that shows to whom the participation belongs. No comma is needed. Treat matches its plural subject staff. Options (4) or (5) would destroy the parallel structure in the sentence.

8. **(1) injured, but** (Mechanics/Comma Use) Option (1) is correct because a comma is needed between independent clauses joined by a conjunction. Options (2), (3), (4) or (5) do not provide the needed comma and introduce other errors.

9. **(2) on an apartment balcony, barbecuing** (Sentence Structure/Fragments) Sentence 2 is a sentence fragment that needs to be attached, with a comma, as an dependent clause to the independent clause (sentence 3) that follows it. Option (1) omits the comma necessary after balcony. Options (3), (4), and (5) insert inappropriate connecting words.

10. **(3) fish, vegetables, and breads** (Sentence Structure/Parallel Structure) Only option (3) is parallel in structure. All other choices are not parallel.

11. **(3) replace it with them** (Usage/Pronouns) it refers to a plural antecedent (wood chunks, chips) and should be replaced with the plural pronoun them. Before expresses the right time to soak the chips. The comma is necessary to separate the dependent clause from the independent one that follows it. No comma is needed after water.

12. **(1) grapevines and herbs that lend** (Usage/Subject-Verb Agreement) Grapevines and herbs is a plural subject that matches lend. The other options use singular verb forms that do not match the plural subject or are not in present tense.

13. **(2) replace its with it's** (Mechanics/Possessives & Contractions) The contraction it's is needed. Have matches the plural subject grills. No other commas are needed.

14. **(2) smoke if meats are** (Usage/Verb Use) Only option (2) has correct punctuation and a plural verb to match the subject meats.

15. **(4) breads should be grilled over** (Usage/Verb Tenses) Option (4) supplies the necessary verb form.

16. **(2) with sentence 5** (Organization/Dividing Paragraphs) Sentence 5 begins the how-to tips section. None of the other options creates effective text division.

17. **(2) insert is after popcorn** (Sentence Structure/Sentence Fragments) Only option (2) provides a singular verb to match the subject popcorn. The comma changes in options (1) and (4) are not needed.

18. **(1) in Chicago, Americans buy** (Sentence Structure/Fragments) The combined sentence is: "According to the Popcorn Institute located in Chicago, Americans buy over 800 million pounds of unpopped popcorn each year." The other choices do not clearly convey the meaning.

19. **(4) ingenuity, a new way to pop** (Mechanics/Comma Use) A comma is needed after an interrupting phrase. Option (1) does not make sense. Option (2) is incorrect because no comma is needed. Options (3) and (5) use incorrect verb forms.

20. **(1) change Brothers to brothers** (Mechanics/Capitalization) Brothers does not need to be capitalized. No commas are needed in this sentence. Have matches the plural subject brothers.

21. **(3) has been changing** (Usage/Verb Tense). Only this verb tense (singular present progressive) works in this sentence and agrees with the singular subject it.

22. **(1) change are to is** (Usage/Subject-Verb Agreement) Is matches the singular subject ear. The comma after oven separates two clauses. The comma after white separates two adjectives. No other commas are needed. There is no verb bursted.

23. **(5) appear before their eyes** (Usage/Pronouns). The correct pronoun to refer to the word people is their. Options (1) and (2) use incorrect verb forms.

24. **(1) with sentence 5** (Organization/Dividing Paragraphs) Sentence 5 begins a series of sentences about the brothers' new product. The sentences in options (2), (3), (4), and (5) are details within the paragraph.

25. **(3) remove sentence 13** (Organization/Unity & Coherence) Option (3) correctly eliminates a sentence that does not support the main idea of the paragraph. Option (1) removes the topic sentence. Option (4) removes a supporting detail, and option (5) removes an effective closing.

26. **(4) replace personal with personnel** (Mechanics/Homonyms) Personnel (employees) is the correct word. None of the other options makes sense.

27. **(3) Everyone is invited** (Usage/Subject-Verb Agreement). The singular subject everyone takes a singular form of the verb, is. The other options use inappropriate verb forms or do not address the subject-verb agreement.

28. **(1) Here are some of the ways you can check up on your health at the fair**. (Organization/Topic Sentence) This is the only option that offers a reasonable topic sentence for this paragraph.

29. **(3) test your blood pressure and talk to you** (Sentence Structure/Parallel Structure). Option (3) makes the two verbs test and talk parallel in structure. The other options do not create parallelism.

30. **(4) cholesterol, considered by many to be** (Sentence Structure/Subordination). Option (4) uses a comma to attach a dependent clause modifying cholesterol to the end of sentence 6. Option (1) creates a run-on sentence. Option (2) creates a comma splice. Option (3) uses an incorrect verb form. Option (5) requires a comma to be correct.

31. **(3) turnout will top** (Usage/Verb Tense) Option (3) correctly uses the future tense. All the other options use incorrect tenses.

32. **(5) no correction is necessary** (Mechanics/Spelling) The sentence is correct as written.

33. **(4) with sentence 15** (Organization/Dividing Paragraphs) Only sentence 15 starts a new topic, the closing remarks of the memo.

34. **(5) replace counciling with counseling** (Mechanics/Homonyms) Counseling is the correct word for this context. Writing, response, and peer are used correctly. Days of the week are always capitalized.

35. **(3) position and am** (Sentence Structure/Comma Splice) Option (3) adds a connecting word. Option (1) is a comma splice, and option (2) creates a run-on sentence. Options (4) and (5) insert inappropriate connecting words.

36. **(5) myself. I** (Sentence Structure/Run-on) The run-on sentence is corrected by putting a period between the two independent clauses. Options (2) and (4) insert connecting words that do not make sense. Option (3) creates a comma splice.

37. **(5) replace quiet with quite** (Mechanics/Homonyms) Quite is the correct word in this context. Option (1) removes a helpful connecting phrase. Option (2) inserts an unnecessary word. A comma is not needed after training, and the comma after parents should not be deleted.

38. **(3) other countries. They** (Sentence Structure/Comma Splice) Option (3) corrects the comma splice by forming two separate sentences. Option (2) creates a run-on sentence. Options (4) and (5) insert inappropriate connecting words.

39. **(2) such as these, I** (Mechanics/Comma Use) A comma must follow a dependent clause at the beginning of a sentence. Option (3) creates a sentence fragment. Options (4) and (5) insert inappropriate connecting words.

40. **(3) remove sentence 6** (Organization/Unity and Coherence) Sentence 6 is a tangent and does not belong in the paragraph. Options (1) and (2) remove an appropriate topic sentence. Options (4) and (5) change a logical order.

41. **(3) replace <u>principle</u> with <u>principal</u>** (Mechanics/ Homonyms) Option (1) uses faulty sentence construction. No additional commas are needed.

42. **(3) I will contact** (Usage/Subject-Verb Agreement) The singular subject <u>I</u> takes the singular form of the verb <u>contact</u>. The other options use incorrect verb forms.

43. **(3) life may be taking** (Usage/Verb Tense) Only option (3) is in present tense, which matches the rest of the text.

44. **(3) change <u>Doctors</u> to <u>doctors</u>** (Mechanics/ Capitalization) In this sentence, <u>doctors</u> is a common noun that does not need to be capitalized. No commas are needed. The names of countries are always capitalized. <u>Because</u> would be incomplete without <u>of</u>.

45. **(2) ignored, and your body is** (Sentence Structure/Subordination) The combined sentence is: "When you're under stress, good eating habits are often ignored, and your body is depleted of essential nutrients." The other options do not clearly convey the meaning of the sentence.

46. **(4) up your bodily** (Usage/Pronouns) The entire passage uses the form <u>your</u>. No commas are needed. <u>Additional</u> is used correctly. The revised sentence is: "Stress also makes your body secrete additional hormones which speed up your bodily functions."

47. **(2) rate and breathing rate** (Sentence Structure/ Parallel Structure) Only option (2) puts the two elements (<u>heat rate</u> and <u>breathing rate</u>) in a parallel form.

48. **(4) feel more energetic** (Sentence Structure/ Parallel Structure) Only option (4) uses a structure that is parallel to <u>lower your stress level</u>.

49. **(4) with sentence 12** (Organization/Dividing Paragraphs) Sentence 12 begins a series of sentences on different ways to relax.

50. **(1) It's important to find** (Sentence Structure/ Sentence Fragment) Only option (1) creates a sentence with a subject and a verb (<u>It is</u>).

Language Arts, Writing, Part II

	1 Inadequate	2 Marginal	3 Adequate	4 Effective
	Reader has difficulty identifying or following the writer's ideas.	**Reader occasionally has difficulty understanding or following the writer's ideas.**	**Reader understands the writer's ideas.**	**Reader understands and easily follows the writer's expression of ideas.**
Response to the Prompt	Attempts to address prompt but with little or no success in establishing a focus.	Addresses the prompt, though the focus may shift.	Uses the writing prompt to establish a main idea.	Presents a clearly focused main idea that addresses the prompt.
Organization	Fails to organize ideas.	Shows some evidence of organizational plan.	Uses an identifiable organizational plan.	Establishes a clear and logical organization.
Development and Details	Demonstrates little or no development; usually lacks details or examples or presents irrelevant information.	Has some development but lacks specific details; may be limited to a listing, repetitions, or generalizations.	Has focused but occasionally uneven development; incorporates some specific detail.	Achieves coherent development with specific and relevant details and examples.
Conventions of EAE	Exhibits minimal or no control of sentence structure and the conventions of EAE.	Demonstrates inconsistent control of sentence structure and the conventions of EAE.	Generally controls sentence structure and the conventions of EAE.	Consistently controls sentence structure and the conventions of Edited American English (EAE).
Word Choice	Exhibits weak and/or inappropriate words.	Exhibits a narrow range of word choice, often including inappropriate selections.	Exhibits appropriate word choice.	Exhibits varied and precise word choice.

Reprinted with permission of the American Council on Education.

LANGUAGE ARTS, WRITING, Part I

Name: _____ Class: _____ Date: _____

○ Simulated Test A   ○ Simulated Test B

1 ① ② ③ ④ ⑤	11 ① ② ③ ④ ⑤	21 ① ② ③ ④ ⑤	31 ① ② ③ ④ ⑤	41 ① ② ③ ④ ⑤
2 ① ② ③ ④ ⑤	12 ① ② ③ ④ ⑤	22 ① ② ③ ④ ⑤	32 ① ② ③ ④ ⑤	42 ① ② ③ ④ ⑤
3 ① ② ③ ④ ⑤	13 ① ② ③ ④ ⑤	23 ① ② ③ ④ ⑤	33 ① ② ③ ④ ⑤	43 ① ② ③ ④ ⑤
4 ① ② ③ ④ ⑤	14 ① ② ③ ④ ⑤	24 ① ② ③ ④ ⑤	34 ① ② ③ ④ ⑤	44 ① ② ③ ④ ⑤
5 ① ② ③ ④ ⑤	15 ① ② ③ ④ ⑤	25 ① ② ③ ④ ⑤	35 ① ② ③ ④ ⑤	45 ① ② ③ ④ ⑤
6 ① ② ③ ④ ⑤	16 ① ② ③ ④ ⑤	26 ① ② ③ ④ ⑤	36 ① ② ③ ④ ⑤	46 ① ② ③ ④ ⑤
7 ① ② ③ ④ ⑤	17 ① ② ③ ④ ⑤	27 ① ② ③ ④ ⑤	37 ① ② ③ ④ ⑤	47 ① ② ③ ④ ⑤
8 ① ② ③ ④ ⑤	18 ① ② ③ ④ ⑤	28 ① ② ③ ④ ⑤	38 ① ② ③ ④ ⑤	48 ① ② ③ ④ ⑤
9 ① ② ③ ④ ⑤	19 ① ② ③ ④ ⑤	29 ① ② ③ ④ ⑤	39 ① ② ③ ④ ⑤	49 ① ② ③ ④ ⑤
10 ① ② ③ ④ ⑤	20 ① ② ③ ④ ⑤	30 ① ② ③ ④ ⑤	40 ① ② ③ ④ ⑤	50 ① ② ③ ④ ⑤